# *Poetic Affusion*

– JASON –

An environmentally friendly book printed and bound in England by
www.printondemand-worldwide.com

PEFC Certified
This product is from sustainably managed forests and controlled sources
www.pefc.org

This book is made entirely of chain-of-custody materials

www.fast-print.net/store.php

Poetic Affusion



ISBN 978-178035-393-7

First published 2013 by
FASTPRINT PUBLISHING
Peterborough, England.
Printed by Printondemand-Worldwide

# *Contents*

# *Dedication*

To the lullaby memories of my ever loving mother

***Margaret***

***My Teachers***

***My Family***

***My Friends***

# *Acknowledgements*

Several people I am indebted to for having this first collection of my poems getting published. When I first wanted to share my poems, I was so burdened with doubts whether my poems met the basic tenets of poetry and whether I had the core attributes one ought to master in order to progress to being a poet. It is here the talent spotters or well wishers in every walk of life come into the picture to make artisans and craftsman out of ordinary beings – like me.

In this line of early admirers and encouragers of my poems come my dear friend, colleague and soul mate Mark who knowing me to the last cell of my body and to the core faith of my soul; sent me very encouraging comments on my early poems. Soon followed several including my close friends Sylvie, Aru, Graham, Kiru, Ravee, nephew Nigel and cousin Rev.Thani.

I also must not fail to record others who instilled poetry in my life. My English teacher from Sri Lanka Mr.Alvinus who so passionately taught a selected few of us in our class, the tools of poetry to take wings with my teenage illusions, infatuations and imaginations.

I must also acknowledge my bold and brave friend Graham for continuously publishing my poems of critical content on governance of Britain on the National Liberal Party website. Also I am grateful to the United Press for publishing couple of my poems in their anthologies of 2010 and 2012.

Last but not least to the publishers at Fast Print Publishing, especially Pauline, Nicky and Marika for patiently going through the motions of putting together a novice's writings into a book form.

# *Introduction*

The collection of poems by Jason in this book, in their multiple ranges of ambience and shades, present his inner aching to write poetry; not just for the sake of publishing a book of poems; instead to use his poetic skills to bring poems of sentiments, topics, people and places to the poetry-reading community worldwide.

His poems raise a fundamental question of whether a poet is naturally endowed with poetic skills or one is crafted by the poetic and linguistic traditions and environments with which one gets born and lives within? His poems of dreams, romance, infatuations, disappointments, rage, fear, guts, wit and scepticism were all shaped by the people, places, prejudices, pleasures, values, beliefs, tradition and faith into which he was born, lived, dreamed of and aspired for.

His inspiration for writing poetry starts with the most loving admiration for his mother. Through his poems, he embraces the beautiful coastal line of sun-draped sandy beaches, cooling sea breeze, bright and long days of sunlight and unfailing monsoon rains in his scenic native village called Palaly in Sri Lanka. And indeed some of his poems reflect the village in which he grew up in its naked, yet colourful, presence then and its destroyed and destructed state now.

Reading his poems, one senses a rebellious voice against the social, political and racial prejudices which the world is riddled with. His experience of the caste-ridden social prejudices he lived with; and the political prejudice for being part of an ethnic minority in Sri Lanka which he experienced first-hand; and his in-depth knowledge of a struggling nation (Tamils in Sri Lanka) for parity, equality and justice within Sri Lanka; all of which provided him with the passion and knowledge to write poems of extraordinary emotions and humility.

His personal experience of racial attacks, on at least a couple of occasions, on the streets of East London in the "paki-bashing" Britain of the early 1970s provided him with an acute level of self-consciousness and awareness to paint such experiences into poetry. His acknowledgement of such realities made him volunteer as a political and human rights activist to work amongst London-wide immigrants and refugee communities of African, Asian, Latin American and Middle-Eastern origins. All these very valuable experiences have left their lasting imprints on his thoughts and writings.

The extraordinary courage demonstrated by the people of his village, despite their lives bordering poverty; very vividly left their impressions on him to feel emotionally attached to the plight of ordinary people. And through his extensive travels in Asia and Africa, he also witnessed the cruel twist of poverty which touched his soul to transcribe ordinary people's sufferings into poems to voice his protest at this curable curse which humanity continually allows to prosper.

Some of his poems make the strongest possible protest and stand in defiance of poverty, malnutrition, war, state terror, discriminations, ill-health and violence based on ethnicity, language, religion, caste and sex; and the sheer hypocrisy he found in world politics and diplomacy. Some of his poems illustrate his appreciation of individual or collective courage of people and their community.

They make bold and emotional statements on anti-war to green perils; knife crimes to the abuse of children and women. From exploring the self and the soul, to recording special moments of history; to dissecting and exposing the hypocrisy buried within politics and diplomacy; his poems also inspire and mourn the death of very special human beings.

Jason takes pride in having been anchored on poetry from his linguistic and cultural home, Asia. Equally he is proud too of the poetical, linguistic and cultural traditions of his acquired home, Britain. Like two merging tributaries bringing power, richness, momentum and strength to a river, two divergent linguistic and poetical traditions to which he was exposed to have enormously enriched his poetic skills and techniques.

Much as he acknowledges the ever-inspiring character and contributions of people and the environment surrounding him to write poetry; his poems also acknowledge the ever-inspiring influence of world events, issues which touched his heart and the topics which his soul urged him to poetically make notes about. In summary, his poems are defiant statements and a collection of critical perspectives on a range of current topics affecting ordinary people in their extraordinary lives.

To his credit, some of his poems have appeared in websites (National Liberal Party, State of Minds) and United Press's anthologies published in 2010 and 2012.

It seems poetry is a soul within his soul; it romances, inspires, embraces, triggers, rages, soothes, paints, cries and touches him in the most intricate forms. Therefore it is most appropriate to say that poems found in these pages are his humble offerings to the millennium's old 'Great Art' called poetry. Through publication of his poems he also receives humbly his baptism in poetry.

# *Hymns to Mums*

Mum - Blessed heaven her origin,
Womb we lived where love nest-in
Sum of blessings buried in her smile,
Roomy heart her's, which spans for mile(s).

God's presence she in our midst,
Shades several may she take, yet sweet.
No pomp when her embrace reach
Out to extend warmth - her love never breach.

Quilted well we, by the warmth of her bosoms,
Children drain them until hind milk arrives.
Bearing pain of bitten nipples and aching body,
Feeding mums-benevolence in total embody.

Your bosoms, our cushions, where we buried,
Sorrows endless, and woke afresh, woes relieved.
Browsing us afar, fore-guesses she our pain,
Stars do oblige and descend to please her kin.

Own dreams for morrows, never she dreamt,
Dreams of our morrows which drove her prompt,
Streams of all her endeavours centred on children,
Like beam-stuck night flies on glass of lantern.

Sleepless, kids of aches and infirmities,
Disturbed by demons or for infant calamities,
Night vigils countless by verandas and poaches
Kids impose; mums dispose-dedication her mental riches.

Pain or pleasure, she walks supreme over emotions
Rain or shine, she reign by the gift of her womb
Rich or poor, her bosoms see no discriminations
Ditch her and yet her love follows us beyond her tomb

*Jason*

Soil feed us all, for sake of buried mums,
They seed and nourish earth from their tombs,
Sky rain aptly all seasons, sign of mums yet to come,
Praise be to mums through these humble hymns.

# *The Thinning Line (Lane) into the Unknown*

Oh God! What a wonderful gesture
You the almighty provide
To humans - the gift of life to stride
Into the earth, each with a unique caricature!

Life begins at the summit of emotions,
And ends by the escaping spirit of the heart.
Between pleasure and pain filled commotions,
Life is like an in-flight bubble about-to-burst.

By the spring seasons of life,
Only the green valleys and meadows;
The prowling eyes choose to shadow,
Avoiding the dead leaves and brown boughs of strife.

At the summit of summer seasons,
Sumptuous moments seem forever;
Slump to follow escape reasons,
Pomp in prime though soon to wither.

Autumn grey creep in to the wings,
Omen abound of twilight to surface.
Slow decline descend to embrace
The life that soon to detach strings.

Winter of life when coldness of people around
Sink into the senses - past debts do not bind.
The minds of small hearts who yet to be matured.
Seed of discontent and woes soon shall have them captured!

*Jason*

# *A Dead Poet and Wild Red Rose*

Walked, the lord almighty one morn,
Along a pathway seemed a garden.
Plants, leaves and scrubs all brown,
Stood in their fierce nature torn;
Unveiling to the lord the burden
Once ever so lush green garden had been,
Through the summer that had little rain.

Frowning over nature's dethroned
State, God, the graceful set his eyes upon
A lonely wild red rose standing in crowning
Glory of red-cheeks, like a queen.
Petals slightly dull yet bonnie,
Leaves and stems a patchwork of pain.

Knelt the lord, by the queen of garden
Gently reaching and humbly prodding
The beautiful wild rose, with the hands of healing
And asked the Lord: How you survived the scorching
Heat which swept this lush green garden?

My lord, replied the wild red rose,
Beneath me rest a poet not well known,
Who recited lyrics and poems in the evenings,
While he watered this garden for many years long.

He who was generous to this garden gone sky way,
And no soul to wet this pathway.
Wetness of his remains beneath by which I thrive,
And richness of his verses and rhymes in the air still pass by!

# *18 May 2009*

Dreams of an ancestral nation,
Destroyed in bloodied conclusion,
Chilling cries of thousands put to death,
By a willing coalition of nations through deceit,
Saints and Satans of just divide joined hands,
For wilful genocide by a dictator's commands,
So shall read the history for generations to come....

Three square miles of killing stretch,
Therein cornered half a million in genocide siege;
Days went by while norms of war took breach,
Heavily on defenceless civilians; the besiege
Of hungry, thirst, wounded went on while justice slept
On laurels of global leaders; while truth in silence wept,
So shall read the history for generations to come....

Come shall times for justice, even be they delayed,
Shame shall stick on those keenly devils-way strayed,
Dreams of a nation never get buried for good.
Cream of leaders morrow shall rise instead,
Prime times of history'll turn new pages afresh,
Chime shall bells for a new dawn for those got crushed
So shall turn the history a new dawn for a Tamil Nation.

# *A Prayer*

Oh Gods of Mercy!
Pray, we do solemnly – to
Preserve sanity in thy lands.
Presumptuous vanity blinds,
Precious values of gaiety
Precariously left to decay.
Stray dogs of war gather,
Robed in democratic garb;
In rooms of marble and malice.
Roaming satellites a curse,
Rebelling few against injustice,
Remotely put to death – without
Remorse or repentance.
Weapons of mass culling,
Munitions and armaments of
Mountainous proportion;
Find their way to mass murderers.
To mend these maladies – we
Find no solutions.
Halls of justice remain,
Halls of inaction.
Peace makers' pretence
Pierce hearts of peace lovers'.
Well meaning rights statutes
Swell the halls of righteousness;
Bells toll to pronounce them – yet
Wells they're buried deep in; and
Dwelling in anticipation of them
Be-welling thy land and people a
Bewilderment thy grace!
Thy kingdom come

Rogue leaders and cronies be
Brought to justice - with
Drought infested eyes
Thy subjects – we cry and pray!
Amen

*Jason*

# *A Stroll by the Tea Garden*

Winds over the tea valleys chilled and mellow,
They bounce over the mountains gentle and slow.
Dance, the bamboo trees in romancing motion,
Trounced, the heart in poetic submission.

Multiple incessantly moving streams,
Soak the ground beneath to willingly swell.
Passing grey clouds on travel, often unravel
Pearl rain drops, turning soul to dreams.

Green bellies of hill country cliff tops,
Rife with wild bloomers of varied kind.
Lilies, amaranthine, anthuriums, orchids;
Their colour magic feather the unease mind.

Skeletal, draped in poverty-torn gani sacks,
Women rush up-down the foot paths,
Of tea mountains with head held baskets,
Filled with plucked flushes of tea plants.

At distance, across the horizon rose,
White ash clouds towards the skies.
Beamed a rainbow above the white mist
Of waterfall; eyes glued to this nature's twist.

Across the valley, by the mid rift of the hills,
Moved uphill at snail pace on the rails;
Through the tunnels, over the bridges
The noon time train - Nanu Oya Express.

Rimmed tea hedges amid surrounding crops,
Spread green carpet across mountain range.
Shooting fresh tea flushes crowned by dew drops
Provoke thoughts to new heights of poetic challenge.

# *Aruna I'm not I am now called PVS (Persistent Vegetative State)*

Neither am I alive
Nor I'm dead
Grey lines of strife
Strayed into my life
I am not *Aruna* which I was once
I am now called PVS!

One not fine evening
Prowling man of depravity
Plundered my dignity
Plunged me into nothing.
I am not *Aruna* which I was once
I am now called PVS!

Prisoner I'm of morals proclaimed.
Though I'm dead, death is denied.
Professional ethics keep me alive.
Profoundly I wish to sleep for life.
I am not *Aruna* which I was once
I am now called PVS!

Coma I'm in or no coma?
No one seems to know
Dramas around me routinely follow.
*Karma* I'm slated for which I endure solo.
I am not *Aruna* which I was once
I am now called PVS!

*Jason*

Twenties I was in when PVS trapped me.
Plenty tubes currently strap me.
Skinny and bony, my current state is agony.
Pinning my hopes, so I'm free of this irony.
I am not *Aruna* which I was once
I am now called PVS!

Religion, politics for me of no solace.
Rules and ethics, to me so callous.
Let my spirit depart, ***Aruna*** lives no more!
Put faith aside, help PVS' depart as our backs are sore!
I am not *Aruna* which I was once
I am now called PVS!

# *Bantu Land... Seeks a New Front*

Rise *Azania, Amandla. Azikhwelwa*
We yelled, holding high freedom torch.
Comrades fell when bullets pierced our march.
Yet never entered our hearts the fright!

Freedom we yearned did arrive,
Yet in our midst only poverty thrive.
So we cry as our dreams die in wombs
And our feelings put to the flames!

Tin roofed shacks, salt filled bowels
Pain driven lives, gay void homes.
Drained of hope, tormented our nights.
Through roof holes, stars sigh at our plight!

Poverty, deprivation nakedly endemic,
People killed in preventable epidemics.
Emerging sky high towers pronounced as epic.
Yet expanding *bantu* slumps confirms of poverty endemic!

White apartheid we rebelled against collectively,
While economic apartheid infesting us silently.
Right these imbalances so we may prosper rapidly,
Fright of failing the revolution haunts us unashamedly!

Freedom we yearned, had failed in our midst.
Wake up, the pretentious successors to the seat
Of *Madiba*, freedom earned under threat.
Bring fast equality, to quench our real freedom thirst!

These are slogans used during anti-apartheid campaign
*Azania :* Pan African use of term *"Azania"* for South Africa
*Amandla* : a Xhosa and Zulu word meaning "power to people";
*Azikhwelwa:* Away with bantu policy (separate development policy of Apartheid)
*Madiba* – One of many honourable names for Nelson Mandela
*Bantu* – an official name used to call black South African slums under Apartheid

# *Beauty*

Full moon, my face once,
My presence, floral fragrance,
My hips, dance of elegance,
My lips, renditioned romance.
Coated in sensual abundance,
Missed rhythm, your heart, by my glance.
My deep penetrative eyes -
Set your mind in perpetual trance.
Drunk on beauty eulogising often you dance'!
Oh my lover of weaker substance!

Seasons not many, my darling lover of flesh,
Lasted our romance, soon you began to trash
What once was your pride - my beauty; crush'
You, our love which oft you serenaded; you thrash'
It as infatuation, your ever so evasive eyes,
Spelt doom to our romance; and I sensed preys
Elsewhere have come into your horizon; ties
We knotted threaded by beauty of the flesh- not of souls.
Beauty once I took pride on, became burden to my senses.
Poverty of knowledge sung requiem to my lost innocence.

Wish I'd known, curves and roundness of body,
Fresh face, fairness of skin, cat walk beauty
What you sought, not beauty of substance!
Oh lover of my past indiscretions, credence
Of love live in the soul's chambers of innocence;
Selfless thought, motherly tolerance,
Boundless giving, endless caring and loving radiance
One generate where take abode, real romance.
Much as I am wiser now, depth of my ignorance
On beauty spelt doom to our ill-conceived romance.

Oh the wild chasers of beauty, young and old,
Search not beauty in the exterior; behold
Beauty! Which is beyond curves, colours
Fragrances, religions, race and dollars.
Beauty dwell deep, in the chamber'
Of sensual and vibrant soul…always remember!

# *Behind Barbed Wires....... Languish A Nation's Pride........*

Bold and brave were people of *Eelam,*
Fought to be free, they rode fear of death
Raw guts, did not stand in good stead by them
Crawl they didn't, while bullets pierced their breath!

Oh! Gods of Mercy, cried angels with pity,
Seeing the carnage on beaches of Vanni,
Seeds of shame spilled all over humanity
Blown, strewn across were worlds' morality!

Hearts of steel, stood people against
Armies of several nations lacking moral diligence.
Blood bath of gory details ensued in silent,
Clouds above shied away on scale of violence!

Once proud people of rigour and valour,
Trounced at battle by world of dishonour.
Today *Tamils* languish behind barbed wire,
Heydays of *Tamil* honour in pitiful disarray!

Hands that fed visitors to brims of their bowels,
Hang loose on barbed wires begging for hand outs,
Rancour run deep, pain suffered hard to bear;
Despair in the air, morrows seem bleak and bare!

Land of plentiful stand idle, cracked and barren,
Seasons come and go farms see no plough on.
Ocean farers sit still by beach no fishermen to return.
Soon be straightened, we pray to Gods, this humiliation!

Homes and domes of temples remain bombed,
Humour and piety which filled'em been emptied.
Huge bulldozers bring to ground what still stand,
Burial grounds that honour sons of soil too're desecrated!

Freedom's pride bleeds, watching it hurts our soul.
Mild mannered mandarins of world see no quarrel.
Wild orchids will soon blossom on burial soil.
Riled kids once again shall rebel if world today fail!

# *Being Old Not Always Gold*

Like the retreating wave,
Drained of energy, I stroll
Towards the waiting grave
In my old age, weak and frail!

Youthful mornings I woke, in the past,
Not yawning but romantic and bright.
Yearning now I, for such bullish state
Except for few rare fetes, rest a dream most!

Once prowling brown eyes of glint,
Romanced all eves with Romeo grin.
Old and rinsed of energy, now they sprint
Not to women as no return for the strain!

Promenade walks of assured indulgence,
Predominant then to propagate prominence.
Joints creaky, legs now 've lost their elegance,
A few steps out seem beyond endurance!

Steps to climb seem a heaving challenge,
Lifting weights make the back to cringe;
Swift moves make body to miss the balance,
Drift slowly my soul from the body of no substance!

Door shut and window-less room this old age,
Dark, cramped, vision impaired, no one to visit,
Rotting away this life, too slow to my taste.
Plotting of god not known, anxious I'm for the last passage!

# *Beneath the Rubble and Debris*

**(This poem is crafted in dedication and memory of victims of Haiti Earthquake)**

Beneath the rubble and debris,
Pinned down amid blocks and mortars,
Seconds of life ebb away like decades.
Spooky silence scary except for sounds.
Occasionally heard of slipping bricks,
Caught in this pile of mess lies - my
Mangled body with fading thoughts.

Often I slip into the unknown;
Knowing I'm alone and in silence I bemoan
The dark hole I'm in; broken
Pain provokes a meaningful probe on life;
Which taken for granted by people on the ground
Down here all look bleak and beyond grief.

Echoing sounds of men and machines above.
Trying hard to reach us buried deep - my
Closed eye lids are wet with tears of joy by such
Heart warming gesture of humans;
Yet very next moment reality hit me hard
That seconds of my remaining life fast edging away

Weight above is overwhelming and can't move
Mouth dry fast, a drop of water would do
Breath begins to slump and they get shorter
Death I could feel around and encroaching me tender
Cold beneath needle hard my limps and joints
Air pocket that kept me alive so far begin to crumble

**I sleep .... No....I am slipping.....!**
**Grip of life too abandons me....!**
**Life so precious ..... I slip into the unknown!**

# *Bloody Sunday*

Truth arrived late on goods train,
For those fell at Derry on bloody Sunday.
World took little note of para's fury
Came justice late for the fallen.

Like bloody Sunday in Derry that year,
Bloody days do dawn and end world over.
Oft justice seems never to arrive - a smear
On power of justice – wish justice arrives sooner.

No life meaner to another, so says justice,
But for armies with guns- killing a legal practice.
Into the silence valleys of justice and politics
Do fall thousands to their death - where is justice?

Truth is powerful, preach morals and religions.
Justice in contrast often weak and powerless.
Power of politics over justice often scandalous.
May this world turn soon to fairer horizons.

# *Blue Ocean - Black Gold - Brown Gardens*

Greed of nations and men combined,
Drive search for black gold at ocean bed'.
Royalties and right-to-exploration fees,
Fill treasuries of state and big businesses.
Disasters often a hidden hand in such ventures;
Result - a green nightmare at ocean beds and fronts
Oil spills turning lush greens to oily brown fields
Unfurling brown carpet over blue ocean
Thousand miles span, sea creatures and birds clan
Perish for private-public greed and monetary gain.
Nation states of all denominations can't resist,
Temptation of black gold so they drill and twist
Daggers on mother nature; deep into her veins.
Scale of dogged persistence delivers extreme pains,
Testing extent of mother nature's core patience.
So she explodes to reveal her agony and annoyance.
Oh humanity! What has become of you? whence
You lived with nature in the past recorded no such incidence
And only when you choose greed as a culture
Love for the environ lost and lust of human creature
Reached astronomical heights and thence began sin'
Of global rush to find black gold at depths of ocean
Beg of you humans; your desire
For depraved profits at the cost of depleted nature
Can only lead to blue oceans turning brown
And green lush grounds becoming brown garden'
While earth becoming not garden of Eden, but a burial garden

**Appeared on a web site called State of Mindz in June 2010**
http://stateofmindz.wordpress.com/2010/06/06/blue-ocean-black-gold-brown-gardens/

# *Borrowed Affluence*

Oh the humanity renowned for sixth sense,
Arise to realise the image make up trance
Which you are mired in;
Recall once for the sake of modesty,
Being in a womb void of vanity
You were naked, cramped, on a code hangin'
Branded garments you wore none then.

No make-over, vinyl face lifts or air brushes;
Mere soggy pulp you're in.
Come into the world, affluence crushes
Your sixth sense to be rational;
And veil you into image dimensional.
Like a refugee, arriving from despots hell,
With dignity exposed to the hilt;
We all arrive into this world still
Naked, covered in embryonic dirt.
Just wonder when you acquire the stick
To beat others on exterior image – you hypocrite.

Boss, Ralph Lauren, Locoest and Gucci,
Are brands built by image builders as Sachi's.
Hijack, the PR firms do, your sixth sense,
For your meagre wealth or borrowed affluence.
Come out of this artificial image cage,
And stop making fun of low wage or no wage
Masses, just because affordability is your forte.

# *Charity Within...*

The self acclaimed clever species
Of God; search not amid the riches for traces
Of charity; and instead find it within you,
So may this world be liveable for us all too.

Few hours life, endure the flowers,
Them live to please you, me and others
We humans though, enjoy life of many years,
Yet misery some often seed, a shame on all of us.

Colour of a skin, caste of a man,
Castle one dwelling, tribe one born-in,
Holy book one reading, politics one believe-in
All abhorrent divides, only humans've drawn.

Oh humans of complex interior,
Within you too lie the key to the door,
Of charity often you search amidst the exterior.
Find it and blessed 'll be this world forever.

*Jason*

# *Children of War*

War rape the innocence
And seed hate among innocent.
We, the children of conflict,
Witness the peak that hate inflict',
War maims and kills us- the children in conflict.

Many we're born amidst gun fire,
Most our lives spent behind barbed wire,
Beasts of war, not machines but men.
Scariest to comprehend, world's inaction.
Past to present, war prey on us - the children.

Mined fields often our playing fields,
Killing fields often fill our minds full,
Chilling scenes breed some as future killers,
Kneeling often we pray to end wanton kill,
And having to see this world through wars-very cruel.

Blank blackboards bear our bleak war agony,
Black days among chums, a recurrent tragedy,
Thick skinned, some of us do survive daily.
Rounds of gun fire, mortars and aerial bombs,
Rain on us until we become burial domes.

# *Christmas Back Home*

Mornings, chill with pearl drops
Dew sitting majestic on grass tops.
Hissing sound of southerly wind,
Kissing plants while passing round;
Storming beach front ocean waves,
Filling air with rhythmic sound waves,
Waking to grey-clouds quilted sun;
Immemorial days of Christmas fun
In my once beautiful hamlet of joy.

Sleepy village slow to wake up,
Church bells toll to call for worship,
Kids slung across dads shoulders,
Babies wrapped against mums bosoms,
Rosaries stuck between aging fingers,
Grandpas along with grandmas,
All walk piously to the morning mass.
That was the morning grace
In my once beautiful hamlet of joy

New clothes, tummy full of sweets,
Meaty foods, homes immersed in feasts,
Wherever one goes; welcoming faces,
Embracing loved ones, joyful houses,
That was the way, I remember the x'mas days
In my once beautiful hamlet of joy.

*Jason*

As the day draw to a close,
Sadness comes to the surface.
Another four seasons to dawn,
For this happy day to return.
Sun takes cover behind orange shades,
Moon surfaces above the randy waves.
Street gets darker, yet front of homes,
Adorn colourfully lit x'mas lanterns.
That was the way, I remember the x'mas days,
In my once beautiful hamlet of joy.

# *Come to Mummy, My Danny Boy*

Come to mummy my Danny Boy
Mum not too bonnie my sunny Boy
Sum of life late seem heavy my Boy
Somehow ebbing away time my Boy

Times of past, fairly green Danny Boy
Dreams may not all fulfilled, my sunny Boy
Cream of my dreams you dear Boy
Rhymes of nursery, not sweet as you Danny Boy

Love of Pa, I fell for, memories so sweet my Boy
Rainbow days, star you're born, Danny Boy
Brain-gate flocked with love…love my Boy
Love, reined in you, me and Pap my Boy

Seven years' struggle to frame you my Boy
Heaven's gift to my womb - you dear Boy
Havens lately I seek to hide my pain Boy
For your prime seasons, I may not be around my Boy

My body in ruin lately my Boy
Come spring, blooming buds of white lilies, my Boy
May adorn my bed of thorns; yet be strong my Boy
Mamma, never go far, ever by your side my dear Boy

Stubborn I'm, not to leave you so young, my Boy
Soon to demise this wonderful sojourns my Boy
End it has to, yet as you reach heights of life my Boy
May godly garlands adorn you my sunny Boy

# *Constructive Ambiguity in Diplomacy*

Oh! the ancient art of diplomacy!
When and why did enter your womb,
The concept of constructive ambiguity?
Forcing thousands lives to their tomb!

Oh! the ancient art of diplomacy!
Portals of live wire media across the world beam,
The righteous forces to fire weapons free of ambiguity,
Which burn reason beyond recognition; and maim
The beloved concepts of humanity.

Oh! the ancient art of diplomacy!
Being fair not your forte – instead you're choosy.
You choose to intervene for masters,
Who seek business not justice for beggars!
Shame you leave global arenas so messy.

Oh! The ancient art of diplomacy!
Shelter-less thousands seek sanctuary in jungles,
Sympathy-less bandits roam guns held as mantle;
Shapeless corpses line the streets to diplomacy,
Suited diplomats coin phrases of delinquency;
Including that of constructive ambiguity.

# *Democracy on Gun Boats*

Oh nations of global goodwill,
Never again impose you pretentious will
Of delivering democracy to ill
Nations, as evidence suggest you often fail.

Invading to impose change of regimes
Inundated with pitfalls and it's a noble crime.
Do cast your eyes on stream
Of events unfolding daily in Iraq, Afghanistan - a real shame!

Corrupt dictators, terror factory,
Often grounds grandly given to justify,
Interventions in Iraq and Afghanistan
Today burning hell they're among nations.

Billions oil money to be extracted to rebuild,
People lives – pre-invasion propaganda claimed,
Yet billions schemed
Away from Iraq's treasury, under an unaccounted sham,
Iraq of today, stand as a monumental shame.

Neither democracy nor development delivered so far
Fractured state, polity; deep fear and terror
Driven masses; direction-less future - all together,
A titanic failure to the detriment of civilized behaviour.

Above all, moral summit and mission,
Exhorted values, ideological conviction,
All seemed to have crashed, and remain broken;
Scattered pitifully on cynic-laden critical terrain.
So may you, never again, export democracy on gun boats.

*Jason*

# *Deraa (Syria) – The Spirited Town of Resistance*

Stood, a man at the verge of death,
Facing a loaded gun to his mouth,
Shouting at the height of his breath,
Freedom to Syria, Oh mighty Allah!

This, a single image in the town of Deraa,
Amid the killing spree widespread in Syria.
Such loud cries so common in lands of Arab Peninsula.
Oh the Omnipotent Gods – do come and avenge
Such heinous crimes,
By the regimes of Arabian Peninsula.

Images of crimes, cameras have captured,
By spirited efforts of protesting youth.
Yet the imagination of the world not triggered,
For ending this ever unfolding horrors and death.

Listen to the tear-filled narration of Nawal Al Shari,
The mother who lost her dearest son Thamer-
Only fifteen years old, robed in freedom flag,
He entered the fray of wolves and died like a stag.

Oh God almighty, the revolt was peaceful,
Yet unleashed on the defenceless with the intent to kill;
Was Shabiha* and weapons of mass-cull.
Why rulers face no sanctions? God the merciful!

*Shabiha: paramilitary thugs

# *I wish you know.....Darling.......*

Spring bloom,
Shining rays of sun,
Still waters of ocean,
Strumming notes on violin,
Streaming birds on horizon,
All this I loved once.
When your eyes of brown,
Were by my side.
I wish you know...Darling!

Sunday stroll down the park lane
And pranks on park lawns,
Runs by beach fronts,
Melt down behind sand dunes,
Found I, oft my feet off ground.
Kind words many dawned,
Yet in the end, you drowned
Me in tears; mortal wounds
Of those days still round.
I wish you know.....Darling!

Like strolling clouds caught,
In wind storm of a twister,
Fine words and emotions,
You spoke all seems,
Windswept by your long silence.
Mind mull over those moments often,
Yet ending them seems full of pain.
This, I wish you know....Darling!

Crying I, for soul-mate I lost,
Bemoan I, death of our love.
Ruinous days, I spend behind doors.
Roaring loud I do, within;
I try to push you away, yet
Remaining few corners in my heart
Resist such feeble moves,
I wish you know…..Darling!

# *Do you hear me Sweetheart?*

Do you hear me sweetheart?
Cries of my soul which never exhaust,
And the intervening sobs which reverberate
Within my humble heart, missing its rhythmic beat.
Echoing loud, pronouncing the surreal state
Of my love for you dear sweetheart.

Love knows of no virtues,
Like a thief rehearsing a loot,
I shadowed you in silence umpteenth times;
I walked sensually behind your curves,
Seeding poems and verses of exquisite
Brilliance - died many of them, guillotined
By the coward who abode deep within me.

Unaware of my constant haunting,
Your elegance always beamed large.
And I sought sanctuary in your ever flickering
Eye-brows and honey-touched lips; scathing
With rage at not telling my love to you.
My lips go dry when I master the courage,
Words stutter in thoughts, and it's a shame
I can't utter the three words to say.. I love you.

# *Elliot, My Cell Mate*

Hello my dear fellows,
Dawn I'm to be offered to the gallows.
Scared and fearful days all over,
Scars of life deeply sour.
Morrow I'm to be sinned - yet
Tearfully I swear, I didn't sin.
Fateful casting of dice -
I'm a victim of justice.

Elliot, in this eight by four rat hole,
Encountered I your caring soul.
What a delightful friend you'd been?
In these memorable months of thirteen,
Not a single day you failed to inspire,
The tortured life I had to endure.
Despite your own strife,
On you I unburdened my life,
Respectable friend, I part you with deep grief.

When my morrows looked bleak,
Will to struggle on seemed weak,
Soon to embrace the rope brought sweat-ful fright,
Kinship you offered was soothing to my heart.
Grateful I'm; your entry at the finishing part
Of my life seem to bring the love I long lost.
May the criminal statutes soon one day
Do away with ropes, so no innocent man ever have to die!

# *English not my mother tongue..... Nor am I a poet of reputable standing....*

English your mother tongue?
Questioned professor Young.
Hundred eyes turned on me - stung
By ridicule, my ethnic pride hung in shame;
High on the walls of poetry's hall of fame.

No, English not my mother tongue!
Nor is it my father's generous giving.
Flourishes in heart where there's feeling'
Streams of thoughts come flowing
Throwing lights on to my inner aching'.

No, English not my mother tongue!
Yet it's the language that I choose loving,
Coming of age in it took me so long.
Call me "Tanglish poet" - nothing wrong
Yet, write I shall until the day I'm dying.

No, English not my mother tongue!
Great mind mine not, humble string'
Full of soulful odes I want to sing,
In submission at the feet of great writing'
Of poets of yester years, since the beginning.

No, English not my mother tongue!
Ills, pains, hypocrisy and plain wrong'
On people with less power bring
Fire in my belies, rebel flames burning,
That's my origin and reason for writing.

English not my mother tongue…!
Nor am I a poet of reputable standing…!

# *Euphemism of Modern State*

Be warned!
To-the-core democrats;
Beyond the business of states,
Beneath the realm of articulated facts;
Beasty tentacles of elites' interests,
Do build a web of euphemist state;
Which a common man understands much not.

Bent on war, psychotic demagogues,
Stand as law-abiding democrats.
They rent state and street media to front,
Make-belief lie torrent;
Amid people with variant
Survival issues to confront.

Elected regimes of smart tyrants,
Plot wars for bogy speculative interests.
Glut of weaponry perpetrate murder,
Beyond humanists tolerance border.
Blood of masses turn to river,
While lies painted world over.

State, a source for seeding cataclysm.
Secret, its weapon for wheeling mayhem.
Pretends, it oft to transcend values noble,
Prevents, it shall at any cost the rebels
Who expose state's desire to be cruel
Towards other states; and also to its own people.

Sleep in bed with this state machine,
A range of entities to cash-in
For power, wealth and position.
Embedded journalists who see no truth,
Ennobled diplomats who propagate myth,
Empty nationalist rhetoric bring wrath,
To empathy-lost masses who are pushed to death.

To be violent, in-built in all states,
To change it, rest on us all democrats.
Until a dawn of such change do come,
Blood thirst world shall aimlessly roam.

# *First Love*

First love our mums, an angel on earth,
Spirit of radiance, her eyes full of warmth,
Envelop us she in cuddles, offering her bosom,
So begins first moments of our earthly blossom.

Infant memories all, about mum,
Intervention of fathers, only some.
We crawl on all fours, she extend her arms.
Seeing first steps, gladden she exalt in joyful hum.

As we walk, no end to mischief, we've her tired,
Kisses, candies and toys, rewards plenty she offered.
Plenty recesses on her lap, memories so vivid in mind.
Love, pride, care, patience all our mums; and she so kind.

Holding her sari's end, endless walks, all day along,
Amidst tiring chores of washing, cooking and feeding;
Angel of safety, she walked behind shadowing.
Beautiful mums, oft we fail to say so while she's living.

# *Five Elements*

**FIRE**

Your romantic glance or casual stare,
Triggered my dormant desires to fire
The flames thus blazed do oft scare
My wits, yet to love so rare
A beauty as you, willingly, dare
I submit my body to a funeral pyre,
Which you ...you alone should fire.

**EARTH**

Your patience, like the mother earth,
Rightly plaudit worthy; my breath
Oft fondly sink into the depth
Of wonderment, as to how your birth
Has so richly endowed you with
Such a wonderful gift of mirth.

**SKY**

Your benevolence, beyond that of the sky.
Even in my bleakest moments, never you shy
Away from drenching my soul or dry
Me with warmth for me to flourish; sly
Never in your make up; much as you try
To be bonnie; promptly tears do cloud your eyes.

**WATER**

You cleanse and quench my thirst.
Like all mums, along you came, the purest
Of the beings around me. In the weakest
Moments of this wretched life, your loveliest
Faculties stood by me loyally. The trust
You showered me, reached the deepest
Corners of my soul and thanks to you, I'm the merriest.

## AIR

In your generous presence I breathed life,
Likewise, when you leave shall come my demise.
Like the breeze penetrating caves to promise
Life to all beings, through the corridors of love
Entered, you to lease a new life to me. With you I rose
To new heights and without you, the poise I possess, I shall lose.

# *Fountain of Poetry*

Feeding mum's face aglow,
Breast swells for milk to flow.
Crying baby content and smile,
Soul aches and lullabies stream;
For a baby in a mother's bosom.
That is fountain of Poetry.

Distance rainbow paint colour on ocean surface,
White clouds fast emerge signalling rain recess.
Silky beach breeze put heart to solace,
Soul aches in ecstasy and so flows
Like a fresh stream, rhythmic verses.
That is fountain of Poetry.

A pauper begs for food on street,
A rich man's affluence belittle such a site.
Decades passed since egalitarian preached,
Conscientious hearts bleed and get pricked.
Soul aches and rebellious poetry flows
Like a fresh stream with rhythmic verses
That is fountain of Poetry.

Heart wrenches at conditions at slums,
State of poverty naked and glum.
To sort this out no heart at helm,
Soul aches to thunderous storm.
Poetry flows with rhythmic verses;
That is fountain of Poetry.

Lofty goals enshrined in treaties,
Shifty moves by strong undo them to shreds.
War, butchery and violence persist;
Soul aches at silkier moves to resist;
Rules enshrined to arrest such decadence fast.
Poetry flows, with rhythmic verses;
That is fountain of Poetry.

Streaming sweat of labour swell the seas,
Dreaming of morrow they forget today's pains.
Conniving bosses reject a reasonable wage,
While CEOs line millions in bonus package.
Soul aches at this naked disparity,
So flows to the full the challenging poetry.
That is indeed fountain of Poetry.

# *Friendly Farewell*

Friends, time with you around
Grinding slowly to an end.
Finding you as my pals, the best
Fortune ever I mustered,
Deep affection tempered
With steeply loyal kinship; your gift, I'm touched.

Having to leave you is painful,
Mark my lines; love to live by you all.
My path, I'm afraid come short of late.
Mindful of that, I state,
Along the way I travel
I shall miss you all.

Journeys we co-travelled multiple,
Platitude apart, you were lovingly incredible.
Those moments were kind and memorable,
Pray I solemnly do, to have you all,
As my friends in all lives
I may have, so adieu my friends.

Plentiful joy you brought my way,
Enriching my days to heavenly joy.
Pleasure filled such moments will stay,
Beyond black holes of galaxy way.
Voyage I'm destined for is hard to sway,
So, adieu my friends of soulful gay.

No qualms, you were all so kind.
Calm while I was enraged,
Blames you owned for my inadequacies,
Seems you found strengths over my failures,
Norms of friendship, I might have broken few, but do
Come to say the last farewell to your friend.

# *Full Moon and Monsoon Wind*

Moon stream spread on surface of ocean,
Monsoon wind monstrously beat coastal region.
Sand dunes blown with hardly any caution,
Mind minces words of poetic passion.

Dancing trees in constant movement,
Sway they do east-to-west in concordant.
Coconut leaves make whirly flight,
Lonely clouds hurry to hide in west.

Mountainous waves rush to stranded shores,
Diligent fishermen, sail to sea adjusting sails;
Belligerent wind push fishermen to edge of craft',
Lighthouse beams swirl from east to west.

Boats on anchored ropes, do medley to fiery wind
Birds not in view to dip in sea with cluck sound
With colourful design, open the west gates of heaven,
The night sky gently draw curtain for bright full moon

# *God's Children Living by Wastelands*

Infants of God live by wastelands,
Depth of poverty, an affront to affluent lands;
Deprived of comforts, them of no one's hands,
Disturbing their living, it burns hearts of decent minds.

Ravaged by poverty, they roam heaps of wastes,
Dawn to dusk, often they fight dogs and foxes -
For spoils of affluence - oh humanity see those babies!
Sacks on soft shoulders, they carry life's hard burdens.

Not apple tart they seek, subtle sympathy would do
Little of what fed to pets could go long to
Settle their disputes with this terrible world - do you
Realize these kids have a right to live too?

While most children enjoy time at school
Wild animals and humans prey on them – a terrible tale,
It could be changed, if humans let their love to stroll,
Few steps along to regain them for morrows world.

They live in dirt, so they inherit ills of all kinds
Thriving ills which, no parents wish on their kids,
Through ills still they roam dirt pits for crumbs,
Because they're scant for what we sweep by our brumes.

Wrote a poet once if a child is ill nourished,
Torch this world as it has no right to flourish.
Breach of such scale of poverty call to search,
Depth of remedies to dawn in a new approach.

So let not children of Gods live in wastelands!
Let world bring'em to a new and fairer land!

# *Greek Tragedy*

Oh the nation of great philosophical tradition -
Cradle once of European civilization;
Oh the home of Homer, Socrates, Pythagoras, Aristotle and Plato,
We pity you, for the gathering grey clouds above you.

Philosophy, logic, ethics, science and poetics,
Knowledge all born amid your critical thoughts,
From times of antiquity, flourished your enquiring thirst,
Today though, changed times burden your economy to burst.

Philosophised once you wisdom to the world,
Plundered now have you all great knowledge of (g)old?
Let not the current economic ignorance
Sink you deep into debt seas;
Instead, let the rays of economic prudence
Pierce through the hanging grey clouds!

# *Hate*

Dormant yet oft lift its head from sleep,
Drive senses to horrendous end-
Death to destruction, hate leads to ends unkind;
Hate - In which mankind buried so deep.

One hates the colour of a fellow human,
Another hates the race of a common creed.
Some hate the toiling of a caste breed.
Within them all a flame of ignorance brightly burn.

Hate, kills infants in wombs of mums,
Hate, burns lives of families in homes.
Hate, erase villages in fire ball bombs.
Hate, end nations in war storms.

Hate gods I, for seeding it in genes of humans.
Hate religions I, for fostering it as a mission.
Hate politics I; for whipping it as a passion.
Hate I all, who bury heads in hate sand dunes.

# *Heart*

Oh my beautiful heart,
How life so dependent
On your merciful effort.
Until death upon you thrust!

Being young loving heart
Prompt all to romance;
Yet being old, frail and hurt
Failings dealt with due diligence.

Oh the heart of generous norms
Amid your veins float the soul;
Calmly you clear storms of all forms
We bring; like a drill.

When organs one after another,
Abandon us to the mercy of death,
Strenuously you strive, like our mother,
To keep us breathing to the end of the path.

Oh my beautiful heart, our last breath,
Your shining moment of glory on this earth,
When you stop, we know you do so reluctantly,
Yet amid your love chambers live life ever so faithfully.

# *Wish I told you Before, Papa*

Hi Papa! Must I tell you,
How much I love you?
Most of what I'm now to tell you,
In the past, never I told you,
Hate I do, of the distance to come in
Between us, on me leaving you.
Sweet man you're, I'll be missing
You dear Papa.

Never I told you, you are my hero.
Fear stricken, I dashed to you.
Dark moments, I slept by you.
Sharp your instincts, protect
Me, you did in all awkward moments';
Like the loving rebel with a flashing sword.
Despite pressing errands, your caring deeds
Kept me in good stead.
Sweet Papa, I'll miss you Papa.

Oft in sleep, I sensed your body odour,
As I woke; I glimpsed your shadows by the door,
My forehead fresh with the warmth of kisses
You just left as I slept. Never there any recess
You left nor I felt of your loving presence
By my side. Oft your built up pretence
To be a strong, hard man; melted like ice
By my slightest show of tearful instances.
Oh my handsome old man, wish I told you all this before.

Oft times, I was awe-struck by your intelligence,
Yet I hated unexplained and expanding distance;
Soon after my body reaching teenage prominence.
Saddened I was for missing that physical closeness,
But later on I understood your fatherly nobleness.
Early hours or mid night calls, you're there,
All year round, in your shadows, I did thrive.
Oh my beautiful dad, I'll miss you so much.

*Jason*

# *Hunger : 1.2 billion*

Affluence hides in shame,
Rich all should take blame.
Radicals may set the world aflame,
As hunger in the world beyond norm.
Lack we all, a collective will to perform,
Conscious moves which shall tame this shame.

Be it may, the world's affluence sky high,
Be it may, the wealth of few word shy;
But one billion among us starve daily,
That should prick our conscience deeply.
Letting such agony prolong - a mockery
Of moral standing we claim to live by.

Starving 'nd skeletal, hunger walk the globe,
Malnourished, kids in despair hung on survival rope.
Food intake face gradual decline 'nd hope
Alone would not save them 'nd we could stop
This sham if palms of our arms reach deep
Into our benevolence, so we gather a goodwill heap.

Underweight, stunting frames, stomachs hollow,
'em walk to graves with tears of pain streaming; shallow
Minds in another patch eat too much and throw
Ample to the waste bins - oh what a bizarre show
Of irony this world witness! Can a new morrow
Dawn for all to be hunger free, so we may end this sorrow!

Access, adequacy, safe food, nutritional content;
Are key issues of note experts oft struggle against.
Success of doing away with poverty seem a potent
Goal; yet war mongers and killing field rogues content
To impose hunger at another level; they make impotent
Of the meaningful efforts of those benevolent.

Mountains of food gather dust in elaborate go downs,
Hectares of lands kept off cultivation in fertile lands,
Policies (CAP) oft justify this wasteful common stand,
While millions starve with begging hands.
Between these vast and wasteful differences
Thrive hunger among the starving masses .

* Common Agricultural Policy (CAP) in the EU and similar policies in the USA , Canada and few other rich nations.

# *Inspiration*

The warmth of your smile,
Refreshed me from a mile.
Bright were your inspiring vibes,
Them swept all my dark clouds – so I scribe.

The glint at me often you threw,
Cleansed my moments of sorrow.
And boundless energy into me grew,
To bounce me to new heights and more.

The empowering waves of your glance,
Inspired all corners of my sleepy posture.
Compassion therein pushed me into a trance
which rejuvenated my sullen stature.

Like a worm edging over to a muddy ground,
Life I inherited nudged me ever closer to you,
Drove I oft into the ground, tired of running round,
Came your goodwill to guide me through.

Oh my friends of ever inspiring charm,
Too little have I told you of your warmth;
Which you showered me all seasons along.
To praise you, I find no verses long.

# *So don't weep Ma, Peaceful I sleep*

Today's sunshine, not for me,
Tomorrows too, never for me.
More days and nights,
Down here I've to sleep;
So don't weep Ma, peaceful I sleep.

Friendly fun drove me to the bar,
Villains knife pierced me to a deep gore.
Still unclear as to what happened there.
Sorrow fill deep your hearts and it's hard to bear.
Yet my dear friends, don't weep, peaceful I sleep.

Hi Bro, To pull me from my last breath,
You did well my dear brother.
Do not dwell too much on my death;
Dreams to be fulfilled for our dear mother,
So brother, don't weep, I sleep peaceful

Hi sis, I do know it hurts - but
My days with you were so sweet
Your love touched my soul, I'm content
Give me five, and watch me touch your feet;
So sis, don't weep, I sleep peaceful.

Mamma, miss your loving embraces,
Warmth of which reach me to these deep ends,
Pranks I played just all seem very recent
Pray I do, to be your son in all rebirths,
So Mum, don't weep, I sleep peaceful.

*Jason*

Pa, thanks for the last tenner under my pillow,
Hope it still remains there.
Take it Pa, have a beer at the bar,
Deeply touched by your love Pa,
So don't weep Pa, I sleep peaceful.

This Poem was written in dedication to the Memory of Ben Kinsella and many youth who die in knife crimes

# *In Your Golden Heart To Serve and Save Others*

***Dedicated to Jordan Rice and Irena Sendler***

Angels of heaven,
Descend to earth of attrition
To motion a lesson on compassion
And they serve the weak with passion,

Like the spring drizzle,
And not like a torrent,
Like a burning candle,
And not like a fire in storming current,
Angels of triumphal spirit
Drop by in twilight moment.

Abode in silence the courage,
Among few to fervent heights.
Who fear not death or envisage
Returns while serving to uphold rights.

Let not courage be judged,
By how many one slaughter?
Instead, be the service which alter
The lives of fellow humans to laughter
Be the tool for heroes to be proclaimed.

Jordans and Irenas
Many in the past and many to follow,
Angels of heaven, in love they wallow,
Which may the mankind follow,
So this world in peace may revolve.

*Jason*

Reaching out to fellow humans - only need love.
Speaking out for the suffering - only need compassion.
Standing out for the defenceless - only need courage.
Delightfully march the serving hearts, to serve other,
To suffer for other, pain they never fear,
Die many for other, that's their finest hour!

# *Life Spectrums*

To be born, not in the hands of one,
Romance or lust, consummate two,
In the chambers of a womb of a mother,
Breed a life to enter the world of smother.

Bound in a miracle confinement,
Begins the journey of to-be-born.
Be it an end in womb's internment,
Or life of grandeur or gutter, nothing known.

Most get blessed in enormity of mother's love,
Foremost to follow, orientation on mother tongue,
Next do follow the imposition of a religion,
Life thus an amalgam of desire and imposition. .

Envious love of mum, stand to good stead,
Caring friends too stand good to the end,
Evolving romance, yet to resolve, to what good,
Revolving life amid these currents, end in soggy ground.

One's season of blooming buds of spring,
To another, fading colours, falling leaves of autumn.
Oh life full of colours, had I known these meaning'
Perhaps, a better human within me born.

*Jason*

# *Travel of a Baby Cloud……*

Like a baby cloud left behind
For pace among giant cloud'
In blue sky over my mother land,
Wandered along I, with the wind.

From distance, smell of my roots,
Fill my nostrils, warn my senses,
Perils of tragedy fill her bellies
Veiled in forced smile, stands
By the shore line, the land of my forefathers.

Enter I, the approaching land front,
Over Palk Strait, rush my heart to reach
The generous belly that bore me; but I can't'
As I am a baby cloud; yet I rush and touch
*Palaly*-the familiar soil-family soil- I love.

Rain drops-my tear drops- reach the blessed soil,
Emotions unexplained, thousands rush within
Search my eyes, candidly in detail',
The land of my forefathers; the soil of heaven,
Kindly given to a handful of die-hard men and women.

Once dancing trees lines - palmyra and coconut
Gone forever. Strong winds of monsoons
Which danced with them merrily off the coast,
Pass by silently in sadness; and sand dunes
Swept by hurrying winds remain motionless.

The waves once endlessly kissed the beach
No more running to the shore line - very strange,
Tiger fish that leapt above the ocean reach
To proclaim freedom, lay dead washed on beach.
Sorely touched, I fetch courage to move on.

Over the old cemetery, I hover and down
I glance, wild daisies and orchids, hybrid cactus,
Solemnly spread over, the half-buried tombstones
Of our forefathers, may god bless them soul;
Weep I in agony, as memories prick my heart.

Barren…barren ….all direction …no homes,
Street once adorned by people and vehicle,
Filled with pot- holes and deep wounds;
Chilled silence fill the street once grandly fille'
With laughter and gay - too much to bear, I turn to pray.

Prayer hall of our village I hover over,
Few stray dogs of war, still hurry through.
Lost of its grandiose tower,
Roof sung to ground, lay in ruins, treasure
Of our village, dreams of our forefathers.

Emotions peak, my eyes sore, tears spill,
Ever there a place to end my sky bound travel,
Here it is, over the land that nourished me well.
So I descend, to die as rain drops on the very soil
I took birth, so bless me god, bless all people of this soil!

# *Lonely and Starving at X'mas*

Shiny 'nd dangling jingle bell',
Them dance on breeze yet not toll.
Plenty 'nd colourful x'mas light',
Them burn but never make life bright.
Hidden in this festive mood, a parable;
Raisin' a powerful question on societal moral.

Across the street, a home brightly lit,
Festive joy bright, a table full of food of delight,
Branded clothes, wrapped 'nd strapped gifts,
Broad smiles worn on faces, free of poverty traps.
Affluence awash while in a corner of one's heart,
Surface a moral doubt as to why so many poor adrift,
From the world of wealth driven comfort'.

Huddled in cardboards, wrapped in papers,
Open to wintry cold, bearing empty stomachs,
Not begging yet living amid abject poverty,
Lonely and deprived of love 'nd charity,
Thousands living amid our affluent vanity,
For whom spare a thought while enjoying the festive party.

# *Love you all.....*

Love you all, not because of
What I was to you, because of what you're to me.

Dark clouds often filled my brain zone,
Yet bright stars you lit my horizon

Right lines never my forte,
Correct thoughts always your fortune.

Like a weed among blooming flowers,
Spike I did your meaningful endeavours.

I like you because you're forgiving graces,
I hate my own self for my past indiscretions.

Believe me for once and for the last time
Relief from my sins to arrive in a short time.

Heart feels heavy with your memories,
Hurt I'm for pricking your souls at times.

Road to redemption filled with terrible pains –
Broad shoulders on which you carried me for no gains.

Frozen heart I have, no blood to bleed -
Like sun descending amid dark clouds, slowly I recede.

Roses would be shy to sit on my coffin,
Bruises I left for you, I hope 'll be forgiven.

Love to buy time, just once to be your shadows.
Your feathers were richer than my soul, my loving doves.

Down your memory lane when you travel,
Frown not by the moments of my betrayals.

Frail I was forever, defect of my genes –
Fragile life of agony mine, there is hardly any gains.

*Jason*

Now it is time to end my sorrows – but do
Note I wanted to say sorry.....Bye my dear ones

# *Mines of Archaic Chill....*

Craving tummy, screaming poverty,
Down men into depth of earth's cavity
Striving to scratch a pitiful living,
Drove 33 men to the point of dying.

Profits may soar for the corporations,
But, never improvements of conditions
For the labouring coalitions,
Despite repeated renditions.

Defying death a daily routine,
Denying poverty a hold, not so certain.
Between death and poverty dangle their life;
Beating them lie behind their daily strife.

Oh brave sons of the Chilean soil
Woes of mine labour may never fill
Your bowels to the brim; instead your soul
To be the price, if mine conditions remain in archaic chill

Fortune favoured you this time round,
Ones you dearly love, alive you they found.
Rejoiced, the world on you reaching the ground,
But obtain apt conditions, before next journey underground.

# *Oh! Magnificent Taj Mahal*

Oh! Magnificent Taj Mahal!
Mere glance at your presence,
Movingly rush soulful romance - into
Mortals of fleshy substance.

*Mumtaz*, queen of love and soul;
Majestically captured her spirit by this Mahal
Minarets, beams jewelled by gems
Moon and stars adorning marble domes

Monument for Love of all times!
Mausoleum for Mumtaz remains! - I've
Kept the promise made by your site - to
Meet you again on a moon lit night.

Many summers passed whence I was here,
Maiden who adorned my young shoulder;
Moon of my romantic castle no more near,
Melancholy my heart filled with and sore.

Most past times run on heart's mirror
Melodies past never seem to lapse and pains soar
Missing her warmth by my side and painful to bear
Mediums' I do search to ease pain and none to fore.

Misty eyes and heaving heart, moment to say good bye.
Moving times may never bring us close - you know why.
Meaning for my life, buried with my angel wife.
Oh! Magnificent Taj Mahal, see you again in another life!

# *Mum, a Bouquet at your Feet*

Generous you were Mum!
Your womb our first home

Caring you were!
Amid biting sorrows,
You nursed us through our pains.

Strong you were!
Stood by our storms
And thorny moments

Proud you were!
Taught us pride and humility too.

Humble you were!
Told us to embrace all with affection

Humorous you were!
We learnt to laugh and make others laugh
Hands that fed us now lay
Skinny and shrunk to the bones.

Infectious smile you had for us
Remain closed and solemn.

Curly hair that beautified your forehead
Remain stiff and uncared for.

We stroked your hair for the last time,
Thinking you might wake up.

We dressed you in sari,
Fulfilling our last duty.

All this on that final day
To prepare you for your last journey

Good bye Mother
For being the Angel you were!

*Jason*

# *Roads I Travelled and My Roots*

Nobody I'm, have no status,
Own no palace, no grandeur castles,
No wills nor any encashment bills,
Nonexistent old man I'm, I down pills,
One too many to survive my ills,
Life at an end, I'm by gates of hell.

Neither have I roots nor roads to origin,
None to claim as kith or kin,
Ruins I live in, I'm owner of pain,
Stains of past indulgence, plenty remain,
Strain I often, as my faculties gone vain,
Mind often fails to stay on straight line.

Hamlet which bosomed me perished,
Mother of mine, deep in gravel, buried,
Lanes I walked, long have disappeared,
School I learnt, dilapidated and destroyed,
Cousins I played with, scattered, some dead,
Yet rousing past memories, occasionally revered.

Women several, came into my life and went,
Most infatuations, rest life-time bereavement,
Children, I fathered few, none to my comfort,
Siblings, got slung far to avoid discomfort,
Village nest-links, war turned them refugees.
Spillage beyond this is of no consequence.

Soon to inherit a six foot mud pit,
High noon for such an end, I can't wait,
Reason to prolong this wretched life-do not exist,
Plenty love I offered, while the return was a tiny bit,
Much as this world revolve around rift and thrift,
Touch of gold I found among my friends, a real gift.

# *My Tormented Soul*

**Like......**
Freshly blossomed Jasmine
Fragrance of your thoughts
Warmly wrapped the heart of mine - yet
Wreaths not bouquets ever I brought for you!

**Like......**
Morning sun rays effect on lotus in a pond
Moving grace of your elegance
Mellowed minds of persons around
Mourn; I do for burning your love for lack of diligence!

**Like......**
Mona Lisa, your heart smiled in hidden abundance
Meanings buried within it filled with exuberance
Mean I was and wish I'd my doubts in balance
More than ever I regret my deep ignorance!

**Like......**
Yesterday seems your presence by my side
Yearning long years since ran beneath the bridge
Waning seasons haven't triggered memories to slide
Woven strings of our past remain highest ridge
Which I can never cross until **my tormented soul** leaves my cage!

# *A Wounded Heart….*

Moon lit night,
We held each other tight,
Rendered poems of aesthetic height,
Our closeness assured heartiest delight.

Resting my head on your spongy laps,
Reading your starry bright eyes
Spent I endless romantic hours.

Exchanged we, few words 'nd more glances
Buried I my sanity into your soul.
Reached my soul heavenly gaiety.
Blinded me your words of vanity.

Yet of late it dawned that
Skin deep was your love.
Ruins that I inherit'd
For pinning my hopes on you.

Spineless heart and spiteful deeds
Several deaths, I survived the lot
Aimless life this now and yet
Kinder world of morrow, soon I hope comes.

Burning amber inner chambers of my soul,
Confine grief there I for a new beginning,
Yet memories of you and times will
Remain in my heart forever darling.

Friend you have found I hope,
Bring all that you wished for,
Yet, if destiny do bring us together,
Pretend we do not know each other.
Pray I do, preying eyes of yours
Never again prick my wounded heart.

# *Nowhere to Hide This Shame...*

Wake up from the pretentious sleep to hear
The pleas of the world poor.
While few bellies line five course meal,
The poor have only water to fill.

Shrink ever their bellies,
Yet prideful, you never they bully.
Amid your money spinning chores,
Beware of the arid land dwellers.

Who see no end to their poverty woes,
For all ages, they die early in rows.
Those living, have no strength to mourn;
Of those dead, no one of merit to mention.

Mere numbers get born to be dead.
More to follow, told, it's God's deed.
Nothing to eat, so they chew rawhide,
From these bare facts, can one hide human pride?

Do you see behind their hollowed eyes?
Turning waves of tears!
No! Because even in naked poverty,
Honour is their most valued property.

Never you witness the poor opening their palms,
Nor do they survive by the meagre alms
Thrown their way; not to them
But to the agents of development scam.

Politicians rest on laurels of mercy bandwagon,
While middle men pilfer crums of millions,
For the starving wealth is survival - not billions
Stockpiled in off shore accounts.

*Jason*

In anticipation of filling, despair the poor man's bowl,
While wild fillings of the rich spell doom to them's bowel
Thus, the reality gap between rich and poor - a shame,
To change this, mankind's heart must have more room.

# *Oh Community of Nations*

Oh Community of Nations,
Come out of your comfort zones,
Cast your eyes on war zones,
As events there will shock your conscience.

The UN club you created,
Shockingly indisposed.
To address volume of crimes
Your partners impose on suffering masses!

Sri Lanka, Sudan, Syria to name a few
Subjugation and sustained violence
On people, you seem to take lighter view!
Is it because value of life lost credence?

Genocide, deliberate starvation by state forces,
Denial of health care, and rights to the masses,
Bombing and artillery attacks on safe zones,
All blow to pieces civilized ambitions for the nations!

Mothers-to-be, infants, old and the young alike,
Butchered for prejudices in business like
Forms; while shuttered minds of the majority stand witness,
Without will to intervene or courage to enforce rules.

Sovereignty concept seems a license to kill; and
Sober unity and sustained silence proclaim a lack of will.
Scheming despots and dictators unashamedly march forth
To put screaming people to unaccounted death!

Ideals of freedom of assembly and media,
Remain worthless on papers they're written on.
Ruthless regimes routinely put down brave
Defenders of such ideals, without impunity.

Until will of nations change UN for better,
UN will never garner the respect it deserves
Urgent call of current times is to alter the course, so
Dawn of respect for human dignity may flourish on earth

# *Oh Gods - Why You Still Hide?*

Oh the moral bastions of religious orders,
In the name of Gods, several of your forefathers,
Inflicted extreme pain and seeded cruel disorders.
The history littered with past such indulgences;
Which shame even the felons of extreme criminal inclination.

Seems these godly mobs never learn to see God;
In the faces of children struck or spiked to death.
Burning schools and homes, to extinct people breath,
The most sinful deeds; godly souls could commit indeed.

The globe today not too different to that of yesterday.
Still schools bombed, assembly for prayers torched,
Death by remote, destruction without trace - the heyday
Of assassins of Gods still march on while love being preached.

The halls of prayers,
Littered with blood of the slayers!
Amid the walls of religious orders,
often hide the murderous leaders!
Oh Gods! Why you still hide?
Behind this tyrannical charade!

# *Oh the West Bound Winds of Monsoon*

Oh the west bound winds of monsoon
Hear for once the torment of a generation.
By the beach side alive got buried thousan',
While fighting to fulfil dreams of a nation.
Streaming tears never dry as the heaven
Abandoned a glorious war of liberation.

Oh the west bound winds of haste,
Like the restless clouds amid your midst;
Memories of the golden past never find rest.
For pains immense suffered all gone waste.
Darling kids of brave mums, courageously fell on dust
Amid the pretence of world of unjust.

Oh the west bound winds of moist
Do sprinkle drops of tears on our bravest,
Whom to the paradise gate we hoist,
With solemn silence and deep respect.
Cherish them all today to rest,
For epochs to dawn, on future generations' chest.

# *Parade at Inhumanity Street*

Men's limit to terror know of no bounds,
A woman stripped and paraded in rounds.
Power, men often wield on grounds
Of caste-ridden idiocy so offends
Women; while feudal justice lay in the hands
Of hounds preying on defenceless women.

Children of god daily pained in Mahatma's land
Current power bearers short change their hand'
Clinging to power seem more relevant to these band
Of jugglery masters; while rights, justice rarely found
As wanted goods; sixty odd years gone by since dawn
Of freedom, yet real freedom evade the down trodden.

Abuse, a way of life in resource strapped village front,
Being pretty - a quality that lead women to descend
Into preying lust-drunk men to pour abusive torrent;
Defiance to abuse, provoke fury of a decadent
Social system to rise in vengeance to present
Extreme pains; yet women survive b'cause they're gallant.

Stripping and chasing women in open - an extreme cruelty
Could culprits wish such an act on their mother or deity
They worship ? - a sobering thought for all men of integrity
And idiots who indulge in such acts of indecent depravity;
While more pertinent line of query should ask ruling elite
As to why and how long more such abuse to be tolerated?

# *Rain Drops on my Grave...*

Even the grave I sleep in,
Have genuine feelings than
Bereaving some of you
Had in store for me.

Tomb I am in more real than
Plumb words many of you spoken.
Room, little I asked of your hearts.
Brooms of deception
You used to sweep me away.

Living among you,
Died I, many a times,
Struck by your cold words.

Blooming buds of roses,
Left on my grave side,
Closer to my soul than
Your perfumed minds.

Rain drops on my grave
Kinder to my soul, I believe;
Than tear drops many you shed
At my grave side.

# *Road to Decay*

Why didn't you walk Pa
That extra mile for me?
Why didn't you make
That extra effort Ma?

Six by four feet dark stretch,
Within it I'm boxed by my own sorrows.
Fixed stare at ceiling of cockroaches,
What I most do in this hell of rogues.

Glimpse of sunlight a rare occurrence,
Surviving pimps and wimps, a fixed recurrence.
In hellish silence, burdened with guilt of crimes
Ending this suffering, do surface often times.

Good and bad, never I learnt to judge.
Mood swings took me to life's edges.
Seeds of sin I sawed have come to haunt,
Brood, endlessly I do to wash hurt within.

Pa, you'd warned me of my road to decay,
Ma, you too told me to sway my way'
Too much of a fool for I went stray,
I caused you pain, Pa, Ma I am so sorry.

Life of crimes, one way street to hell,
A scary downhill chase; fortune reversal not possible.
Moments of pleasure, most vivid on your bosom Ma,
Until I edge to the end, I'll behold you both, Pa.

# *Roses in Turmoil*

Roaring monsoon wind
Pillaged the frontal garden,
Pinned to the bruised ground
Lay the sinned roses of Eden.

Yellow, pink, red petals found
Uncrowned, bleeding on muddy ground
Orphaned, roses are victims of wind's fury,
Unbeknown to them, came their end to glory.

Bare branches of thorny roses,
Bear no strength to look to the skies.
Some bereft of colour, broken lay on dirt;
Left to rot, the end was short and swift.

In turmoil, the roses dear to us all.
Them prevail short on this death ridden soil.
Yet, gracefully them bring pleasure to our soul;
Must not we learn this secret of life at all?

# *Rickshaw Man*

Scorching heat tests his skeletal resolve,
Sweating hands struggle to hold handle bar.
Reeling old pedals often slip and miss to revolve,
Feeling thirst and hungry, rickshawing a survival war.

Looking old, yet not old, that's poverty's hold,
Standing not straight, b'cause his vertebrae tilted,
Rickshawing means - survival of the un-fittest,
This road show often ends at the hands of motorists.

Bowl of rice - only luxury at night,
Bowel he wishes, oft don't crave for food - a wishful thought
Boil his heart often, by arrogance witnessed by road side,
Broiling from humans, burn him deeper than sun heat.

Dawn to dusk, his feet pedal the old rickshaw wreck,
Town to slums, often peddled to feed his stomach
Down a day ill, his family forced to beg,
Gone his youth - wealth of sickness his esteemed stock

Wheels rolling ahead lately become out of focus,
Wheels of fortune never spun him to fortunes.
Wheeling and dealing for daily survival- a routine circus,
Kneeling down often he prays to remove life's curse.

Slum shack of darkness his abode,
Gloom and doom inheritance taken on his stride;
Crumbs in his mud bowl well earned so he's proud,
Dreams to despair cohabit in his shack, yet neither he yawns nor brood'.

# *Shy are you …?*

Hi sky-stuck milky full moon!
Why such haste to seek cover
Behind dark clouds on the run?
Shy are you of lovers' brawl while you hover?

Crying in silence, eves for missing men,
Cheeks of maidens turn rosy pink.
Peeking from above, don't you feel their pain?
Seeking solace they look up to you giant white ring!

Feeding mums script odes of spirited lullabies,
For sleepy infants to've a glimpse of moon on the skies.
Rolling on times register you well in all creatures' brains;
Reeling in lofty praises, sky weeps and rains.

Creatures all have dreamy affairs with you!
Creator thought perhaps your interlude needed too.
Crust of earth, panoramic sky and you in the middle,
So it's written that lovers seek you to have a cuddle!

Ocean front, sandy beach, rolling on waves,
Moon on the horizon while lovers hide behind sand dunes.
Moments of magic, romancing heart so dearly craves;
For big white ball to murmur to the stars, to sing love tunes!

# *So Why Weep Mamma?*

Why weep Mamma?
The life I sacrificed
Was not in vain
Though it caused pain
To you and my dear ones.

Cold breeze of the sea
That embrace the beach I fell,
Endlessly soothe my gory wounds.
Ever moving waves - like
Feathers caress my soul
So why weep Mamma?

I did not die in shame
Neither did I abandon my pals,
Nor did I surrender.
I fought with honour - with
My dear comrades in arms;
So why weep Mamma?

We knew our lives were at stake,
Fell we did bravely; but never did we
Let the flag of honour down.
We choose the path of valour for
Spirit of freedom and liberty to thrive.
So why weep Mamma?

High ideals drove us to the front line
Spiteful enemies we faced in trench lines-
In rows we stood to fight them
Bright young kids we all were,
Fright never entered our minds.
So why weep Mamma?

Right must prevail,
So we fought and fell
We didn't die in vain
Sons of morrow 'll do the same again - Mamma
Do touch sun rays that come through our window
I am there for you Mamma
Mamma, please don't weep!

# *Against Bullying*

Often I cry in silence,
Pain within, I carry in abundance.
The world so often a lonely place,
In dark rooms and corners I seek solace.
Unburdening the pains of bullying
So hard; it haunts me to end this living.

I tread going to school,
For I have no friends only foes.
Like a pack of ferocious wolves,
My tormentors stalk before the kill.
Shivering and shaking, I look to the clock
To rush home; for the ritual again to come back.

Oh God of Mercy, the almighty!
Pray to you and humbly plead,
Strayed I unknowingly into this world
Of hate, prejudice bordering insanity;
May I be blessed just once, never to enter
This world of cruelty; where only animal instincts prosper
While love, like a mirage appears, soon to disappear.

# *Affectionate Affusion "Thalaikoothal"*

Murder camouflaged as mercy,
Humanism's end in ascendency
Parents aged, caged and a spent currency
So, ***"Thalaikoothal"*** - morrow's normalcy

An oil bath to end aged misery,
Affectionately done, no one is sorry.
Altruism strange, siblings kill, to be merry,
Oh Gods of heaven, this crime, where do we bury?

Affluence feeds kids to their pleasure,
While poor starve to fend kids as treasure,
Come autumn, aged parents - a displeasure,
So ***"Thalaikoothal"*** become a rational measure.

Oil bath at dawn, mud drink or tender coconut,
Or force-fed milk to drive the old ones breath out,
All deviant deeds of own children - a dark passage,
In this globally prosperous, yet morally defunct age.

# *Credit Crunch - Spring of 2009*

Spring of 2009,
Came the credit crunch
Banks several folded in a debt rush
Yet the ranks of CEO bunch
Collected millions bonuses afresh
Poor jobs them performed
While treasuries in rows got rescued
Banks front - the customers queued,
For their cash kept for safe keepin'.
Many thriftier money men
Lost overnight their life fortun's.
Canny few though survived the crunch
While bailing treasuries caught in rescue wrench.

# *The Last Despatch - A Eulogy to Marie Colvin*

With an untiring journalistic faith,
Against odds searching for truth;
Prowled this lioness, dictators' war fronts
For highlighting the plight of the innocent –
Marie Colvin, a journalist of truth-bound talent.

Personified she, the unrelenting spirit
For unearthing the ordinary peoples plight;
Amid conflicts unleashed by blood thirst tyrants.
East Timor, Middle East, Sri Lanka to Balkans,
A journey of bravado she displayed on all fronts.

Eye patch clad she despatched reports,
Highlighting the cruel twists of conflicts -
The prime moment coming in East Timor -
Defending thousands of women and infants
Standing as a bastion of hope, facing overwhelming odds.

Marie, this last despatch of eulogy from your friends.
Of war fronts so gallantly you graced from Sri Lanka to Homs,
May the winds of peace embrace and lift
You to the gates of heavens; and among the noble spirits.
May you keep despatching last reports of truth
On the suffering masses at war fronts.

# *The Girl of My Dreams*

Like cool evening breeze coming through a key hole,
Her fragrance overwhelmed my sensual chambers.
Like light rays embracing a dark cellar,
She glanced for seconds over my shoulder;
Graceful figure of beauty and modesty
She impregnated my soul with agony and ecstasy.

Her milky face to my brown skin seemed,
Far distance to bridge, but love conquers
Such differences, comforted my heart.
Her closeness pushed my adrenalin to new heights,
For sensing her beauty at such close distance,
Ever so I am grateful to the Gods of love.

Centrally parted hair, thin white line in the middle,
Elegantly dangling ear studs of pearls and amethyst;
Curled and ever-moving wavy hair by the ears,
Flying ribbons dangling on neatly arranged ponytails
Feeling her presence drove me to seventh heaven, God I
Praise you, you made her on Monday, after rest on Sunday.

White uniform rests gently on her contour,
Bright red school tie dangle on her bosom,
Her ever agile eyes play medley with my
Ailing heart, panting heavily, my world of dreams
Whirl uncontrolled, her eyes, for first time meet my
Weakened eyes, that moment I realized I was reborn again

First words of love, spilled, rather than spoken,
Lost for words, I said "Hello" in hardly audible sound
Fist clenched, muscles tightening, said I "Hello" again,
Fast becoming the man I knew I was, driving
Ghosts of silence within me to sleep,
Thus, I hosted the girl of my dreams to my chambers of love.

# *The Last Farewell*

Prevailed a deathly silence at the abbey,
Entered the family and loved ones to say
The last farewell to the dear relative,
With solemn mourning and overwhelming grief.

Sympathy worn deep on tearful faces,
Congregation soon filled all corners
Of the abbey; legs laden of woes 'nd unable
To conceal the loss of a man to God's will.

Heads bowed, faces buried in deep agony,
Played on the sound system of the Abbey,
The slogan "Om...Om... pounding hearts obey'd
To the manthra, while silence being observed.

Entered the remains of the soul departed,
With wreaths of love on coffin mounted.
One reading Om stood bright at the foot of the coffin,
Pronouncing the religious spirit prevailing therein.

Dark suit, grim face, controlled emotions,
Tensed, facial muscles not hiding inner tensions,
Stood by the crematorium stand, a dear friend,
To conduct the service while struggling to stand.

Hands trembling, fingers twinging,
A few lines on a paper on the stand seem
An epic volume; tears ready to stream
Beyond eye lids - moments for painful viewing.

Grief chokes the throat to a series of hums.
Between the vocal codes and boiling emotions
Painfully caught were the holiest hymns -
*Sivapuranam* – uttered with sacred spiritual motions.

Arrived the last few moments for the tearful eyes.
Grief laden grandchildren expressed love for the old man.
First to stand in a feeble frame 'nd fragile voice,
The grand-daughter robed in shattered emotion.

Word spoken echoed the highest esteem in which he was held
Proud she was to narrate the memories of the past.
The dreams of the old man for the clan revealed;
With pride she wished her granddad, a lasting rest.

Came through the sound system, Om..Om…
For the last time while the curtains in front
Began to draw, for the last glimpse of the coffin.
Thus the last curtain drawn on the life of the old man.
May his soul rest in ever lasting Peace.

*Jason*

# *The Lioness of Myanmar*

Let morrow be the bright day,
When the lioness of Myanmar,
Step out of imposed shackles of tyranny,
And into the rejoicing people of Burma.

Serene yet steely resolve lioness,
Several years behind tyranny's doors.
Yet severe her thirst for freedom
Strength of beliefs held may fulfil her dream.

Strenuous struggles, world do take note,
Strong arms, armaments and brutes,
Stifle never free flowing freedom currents.
Do steer the path to liberty, as the ideal so vibrant.

May waves of people energy rejuvenate
Your tested faith to liberate,
The long suffering masses; let not brutes put to rest
The flickering light of freedom to create
A new era in which real liberty take a deep root.

# *The Ultimate Sacrifice*

None too noble to offer
To the land of our mother';
Than our soul that do suffer
The indignity of the oppressor.

Against strong winds of terror,
Amidst sufferings of extreme horror,
Torch of non-violence we held higher,
Beyond the racists acts of squalor.

Virulent winds of violence,
Turbulent acts of intolerance,
Turned a nation of spiritual peace,
Into an army of honour-bound resistance.

To spill our blood, enemy did choose us.
To kill our breath, destiny did choose us.
To chill our spirit, tyranny did choose us.
To fulfil our goal, our dreams did choose us.

Worth beyond blood our freedom spirit,
Our dreams to be free has no limit,
Sacrifice deter us not; nor pain we'll not endure
Freedom we crave shall dawn-that's for sure!

Against torrent of abuse and violence,
Against currents of denial and indifference,
Against politics of dishonesty and vengeance,
Fought a nation with death as the ultimate sacrifice.

May the monsoon winds off Vanni,
Be kind to our fallen heroes; as many
Decades to come, may them praise the bonny
Boys and girls who fell to give hope to many.

*Jason*

# *God's Children Living by Wastelands*

Infants of God live by wastelands,
Depth of poverty there- a shame on affluent lands.
Deprived of basic comforts, they're of no one's hands,
Disturbing living they endure, burn hearts of decent minds.

Ravaged by poverty, they roam heaps of wastes,
Dawn to darkness, often they fight dogs and foxes.
For spoils of affluence - oh humanity see those babies!
Sacks on soft shoulders they carry life's hard burdens.

Not apple tart they seek, subtle sympathy would do,
Little of what fed to dogs could go long to
Settle their disputes with this terrible world - do you
Realize these unfortunate kids do have a right to live too?

While our children enjoy right to go to school,
Wild animals and humans prey on them - such a rule
Could be changed if world lets it love to stroll
Few steps along, to regain them for morrows worl'.

They live in dirt, so they inherit ills of all kinds,
Thriving ills on 'em, no parents wish on their kids.
Through ills, still they roam dirt pits for crumbs!
Because they're scant for what we sweep by our brumes

Wrote a rebel poet* once, if a child is ill nourished,
Torch this world as it has no right to flourish.
Breach of such scale of poverty call to search
Depth of remedies to dawn in a new approach.

So let not children of Gods live in wastelands,
Let the world bring 'em to a new and fairer land!

** Poet Bharathiyar – A renowned tamil poet from India.*

# *War Crimes Day*

Violet wept for carnage by the beach,
Bullets swept thousands to the ditch.
Bayonets pierced the hearts of much
Of all humanity by the terrible breach
Occurred today $18^{th}$ of May 2009.

Bluff of demons unravelled to of all horror,
Rough injustice imposed full its terror,
Boughs of trees trembled in sorrow.
Love of humanity embraced its death slow
Today $18^{th}$, May of 2009.

Belief in norms of defending the meek,
Got buried amid sand of *Mullivaikkal*★ beach.
Fellowship of humanity ended by weak
Dealings of great nations failing to reach
A dying nation, today $18^{th}$ of May2009.

Today and the epochs to dawn morrow,
18 of May '09 shall be a terrible shame
On proponents of justice; as it's been found shallow
For people caught in democratic sham.
Hence, May $18^{th}$ be remembered as War Crimes day.

*Mullivaikkal*★ *: The beach in Northern region called Vanni in Sri Lanka, which in deathly silence witnessed the genocide of nearly one hundred thousand Tamils in May 2009.*

# *Widows of War*

Oh! Nations of conscience,
Listen and listen fast as our breath
Fast dwindling; our frames are cold
And throats dry; we sleep amid death
Because we are widows of War!

Hate of humans peak in wars,
Machines of war do gory dance,
Crimes of abhorrence staged oft in silence;
Feast of our eyes – husbands and children –perished,
And thus we became - Widows of War!

Hands of evil, embraced us en mass.
Passion of death, forced entry into our homes.
Reason slept fast, while right got raped,
Treason against human dignity silently staged.
Who is there to hear us? We're widows of War!

Dampened cotton, line our starving stomachs,
Yet taunting hunger do not conquer us.
Our feeding hands lay motionless,
Our cookware remain empty of rations.
Yet in dignity we prevail, because we're widows of War!

Strength not there to shout loud of our plight,
Beg we not for rations or foods despite,
Deep sorrow we're burdened with; yet there's pride
In our hearts to demand a fairer ride
At this world of injustice, because we're widows of War!

# *A Loving Grandpa*

Memories agonise deep within to remember,
How long and much did you suffer.
Raw innocence shaped your vigour,
A perfect grandpa you - one could wish forever.

Mischievous dad left his burden – us - on your shoulders;
Moisture heart yours, flourished we under your wing'.
Gist of what I recollect, paint an unselfish being;
Misty and sore eyes, I recollect your silent struggles.

Dawn to dusk errands were plenty,
Drowned in them you did with honesty.
Frowning never, you old man of piety,
Yawning to rest your shoulders - a rarity.

During peak of your suffering, we were kids,
Knowingly ignorant to render you a hand of aid.
Grownups, your shadows abound in our stride,
Proud in the knowledge, we were your pride.

Long years and distance came in-between,
Left you we behind by ocean front for eternal lie-in,
Strong feelings of love you'd for us; they're serene,
So long fair old man, pray you rest on heavenly green.

*Jason*

# *Writings on the Walls.....*

No jobs yet labour do want to work,
More welfare cuts, starve the bottom lot,
Increased tax, the impoverished stuck,
Between heavenly rich and awaiting pit.

Deficit cut seems a holy grail while,
Equity deficient abject poor are frail,
Tight stomachs, not to live but to toil
Until next day's light . Isn't life so cruel?

Tuition fees, no cuts, politicians pledge,
Such pre-poll gimmick to the knowledge
Seeking youth, watered down for privileges
Of cabinet berths, at costs to students and colleges.

Pay freeze, recruitment freeze; labour frozen
To starvation age amidst policies so brazen,
Pushing the labour to a worthless zone,
So the low labour wage may benefit business barons.

No wages, high mortgages, to-rise interest rates.
Negative equities amidst falling house prices,
Biting recession awaits in the shadows,
That is the writings for this kingdom on the walls.

# *Your Honour.....*

This petition I write,
To your court,
With a heaving heart
And soul deep hurt,
On the dishonour
Imposed on my honour,
By a vile brute,
Who is a servant
Of the very state,
You serve through the court.

Crimes on women
Prime assault,
When victors of war exalt
Women cannot protect
Their honour; meekly they had to submit
To crimson deeds which I've brought
To your honour in this affidavit.
I pray, it does not shock your wit!
It ought to challenge your jurist talent.
Hear me loud your honour,
Of the barbaric deeds imposed on my honour.

Different forms of justice,
You and I choose to practice.
Paths differ, but we made our choices.
Justice par excellence - You sought, through the courts
Political justice, I fought for with the bullets.
Path I preferred,
Not my choice, it was imposed.
Under shadowy security inquest,
Holding my family as hostages, I was violated,
Repeatedly by a state official with criminal intent.

No mother of love and sanity,
Disown the baby of her own blood;
Yet, I write this affidavit,
Disowning this baby for guilt
Not of my own making, but
Of that dog who serve for the same crest
Your honour, you most respect
And serve. The baby I refuse to take
Charges for, should be brought
Up by the very state which employed such vile dogs.

My own honour which I hold,
In the highest esteem and regard,
May never be restored through the court
You serve, nor through the very state,
Which allows such crimes to fester
Without due process or justice
For victims as me. Jurisprudence
And practice of it, long since died at the state craft
Of the crest you sit under; so I state
With deep contempt, this baby, though innocent,
Shall stand witness, in years to come, to the crimes committed
By the very same organs and individuals of the state.

# *Ode on Freedom*

Oh the ever rushing time'
Hail loud freedom, for its glory so prime
Of freedom, proudly pronounce this ode
As price highest paid on the road.

Turn the pages of history in every epoch,
Flame of freedom held high with blood.
Sacrifices immensely made by rebels who fought
To hoist high the venerable freedom thought!

Flutter proudly fanned by the strong winds
To the pride of brave men of only fewer lands
The flags of freedom; while in many prisons
And horror states, it endures enormous pains.

Masked leaders with democratic credentials
Task shadowy men of devious essentials
To noose the freedom voice to its death bed
Yet frightened not, even when freedom hangs on last thread!

To ever so brave freedom fighters world over
May the freedom you crave reach you soon!
Unburdened of pains, may the rays of new dawn
Embrace you forever and forever!

# *The End Inside*

Life seems full of sumptuous thrills,
Until from inside it reveals dark perils.
Dwell within, veiled in vanity – the enemy
Living loses meaning as it embroils in agony.

What worth this living?
Amid aches and pains of interminable probing
Thoughts to seek the end often do surface
Which side the pendulum to swing? It's hard to profess.

Rhythm of normalcy gets disturbed
Firm hold on life taken for granted –
Seems a sliding slope to stand on
How true that life is a bonus from here on!

Are you afraid asked a dear one?
Dare I lie as the thought did cross my mind
Laughter I lived by still my shield to hide behind
Softer options to agony rare or none

The end after all is permanent
Embracing it early or late is destiny
Prefaced to be gay to end in tragedy -
That is life in its plumb predicament!

# *Index*

*1.* Hymns to Mums: The most wonderful human beings on earth are mums. Through the poem I want to acknowledge the prime role of mums in everyone's life and submit a poetic tribute to them all.

*2.* The Thinning Lane to the Unknown: The poem explores life through four seasons: spring, summer, autumn and winter. Life begins at the summit of emotions to pass through green valleys of spring, the relentless ascent to the summit of summer, slow decline of the autumn and the season of discontent - the winter.

*3.* A Dead Poet and Wild Red Rose: Poetic interlude dealing philosophically with life, living, death and beyond.

*4.* 18 May 2009: Poem about the last day of the most brutal war of the twenty-first century in Sri Lanka. More than 40,000 civilians paid the ultimate price – their lives – during the final few days of the war.

*5.* A Prayer: This is a critical look at Realpolitik. Some events in world affairs often perplex the most ardent observers. Often injustices are passed on as the norm by the very so-called moral forces who claim to be guardians of democracy, justice and rights while those who fight for rights are often branded as terrorists, for state terrorists to slaughter, without slightest heed to the statutes of rights.

*6.* A Stroll by the Tea Garden: Tea gardens of Sri Lanka have a special place in my memories. I spent many school holidays in the hill-country parts of Sri Lanka. It was both a pleasure and fulfilling to bring the beauty of the scenery into a poem.

*7.* Aruna I am not: This poem appeared in an anthology published in 2011 by the United Press. The poem is about a woman who was violently attacked and raped by a beast. So extensive were her injuries, she has been in a permanent vegetative state (PVS) for the last thirty-odd years. The poem is written from the perspective of Aruna, describing her current plight as well as challenging the orthodox moral and ethical issues faced by the present society on rights issues, such as the right to live and the right to terminate a life. Instead of sitting on the fence on the issue of euthanasia, I take a bold jump on the side of the sufferers' right to terminate their lives.

*8.* Bantu Land Seeks A New Front: *'Azania, Amandla, Azikhwelwa'* was the marching slogan reverberating across the entire regions of South Africa (Bantu Land) during the struggle against the apartheid regime. It is the third decade since liberation dawned on South Africa, yet slums of South Africa have not changed much. This poem is a plea to uphold the spirit of liberation and to address the issues including poverty, ever-expanding slums, malnutrition and poor health which prevail in many towns of present-day South Africa.

*9.* Beauty: A philosophical look at beauty to which most of us often pay heed. Beauty is so commercialised to the hilt that the youth of today think that without beauty, life is not worth living. For many, beauty is looks, curves, shape, colour and dollar and the poem instead locates the beauty within the soul of a person.

*10.* Behind Barbed Wires Languish A Nation's Pride: A prideful nation of Tamils got trounced in a war of liberation and now finds itself behind barbed wire, almost begging for daily survival. A vengeful victorious nation - Sri Lanka - imprisons its own citizens for raising fists in defiance of decade-old discrimination, violence and terror.

*11.* Being Old Not Always Gold: Accepting old age is a big adjustment in life for both sexes. The poem reads *"Door shut and window-less room this old age, dark, cramped, vision impaired, no one to visit".* Painful joints, struggling breath and fading memories are all some of the realities to which one has to adjust from being young, energetic and full of throttle.

*12.* Beneath the Rubble and Debris: A poem in dedication to the victims of the earthquake in Haiti which killed 316,000, injured 300,000, made homeless more than 1,000,000 and devastated the entire region of Port-au-Prince.

*13.* Bloody Sunday: The poem deals with the Bloody Sunday massacre and how justice arrived late for those who died for the fury of a few rogue security personnel.

*14.* Blue Ocean, Black Gold and Brown Gardens: This is a poem about oil spillage in ocean beds resulting in huge natural and environmental disasters as happened in the USA, off the Louisiana coast of the Gulf of Mexico in April 2010; discolouring the ocean to brown and turning shoreline gardens to brown. Behind all this is the greed of investors and oil explorers for black gold (oil). This poem appeared on the 'State of Mindz' website in 2010.

*15.* Borrowed Affluence: The biggest commercial swindle of the 20th century was that of branded goods taking over the lives of people. How the concept of brand names has brain-washed the generations into submission while the PR firms and 'designer' industry combined to turn people into promoters of items for which the customers pay exorbitant amounts of money. The consumer, paying his own money yet doing the PR work for 'designer' firms to make excessive profits.

*16.* Charity Within..: Roses endure only a few hours of life on this earth and yet they give enormous pleasure to us all while some of us live for years spending our lives in hate, discrimination and intolerance, often searching for charity elsewhere while love – the core ingredient for charity - is living within themselves.

*17.* Children of War: "*Blank blackboards bear our bleak war agony...*" reads one line of the poem. Thousands of children perish in all wars and the world often spends more effort counting the number of infants dead, maimed and made into orphans after the war than intervening to protect the children before the war. The poem is a cry from the children's perspective.

*18.* Christmas Back Home: Christmas festivities a constant memory in my thoughts. *"Mornings, chill with pearl drops dew sitting on grass tops..."* That is how I remember the cold month of December as I walked to the church for Christmas Mass.

*19.* Come to Mummy, My Danny Boy: A rhyming poem in dedication to Jade Goodie. As she suffered with cervical cancer, the poem arose as a tribute to all mothers who suffer with cancer or other serious medical complications. Having to leave young kids is an extremely painful process for any mother. This poem, through the verses, conveys a mother's pain as well as her aspirations for a young child she is having to leave behind.

*20.* Constructive Ambiguity in Diplomacy: *"Being fair not your forte …"* We all know diplomacy is immersed in secrecy, deception, deceit, double dealings and outright lies. Diplomacy is also steeped in concepts such as "constructive ambiguity" which means leaving things to be ambiguous and not clear; though weapons which get fired as a result of ambiguous diplomacy are not ambiguous and more directed to kill. Well, such choice in diplomacy means death and destruction to some ordinary people somewhere. The poem explores the roles of the media, portals, journalists and diplomats who are part of this deadly concept.

*21.* Democracy on Gun Boats: From Iraq to Afghanistan, the gun-boat diplomacy to deliver democracy has been a disastrous experience and the poem explores the difficulties involved in such missions.

*22.* Deraa: A town in Syria faced the wrath of Syrian forces for standing up for democracy and freedom. In some details the resistance of the people of Deraa is captured in verses.

*23.* I Wish You Know Darling: A love poem exploring the intricate pains of a lover.

*24.* Do You Hear Me Sweetheart: Unsaid love numbers more than expressed desires. This poem is about an unsaid love… even brave hearts are cowards when it comes to expressing love.

*25.* Elliot My Cell Mate: One of the lines reads "*Not a single day you failed to inspire, The tortured life I had to endure …"* Prison is the most unlikely place for a real friendship to blossom. Yet in this poem a convict sentenced to death finds a cell mate – Elliot – to be his only soul-mate. He soulfully acknowledges that friendship to be his only gain in his otherwise misery-laden life.

*26.* English Not My Mother Tongue: Poetry, *"Flourish in heart where there's feeling, Streams of thoughts come flowing, Throwing lights on to my inner aching…"* Can a non-English person write English poetry? The poem is introspection into my own progress in writing poetry.

*27.* Euphemism of Modern State: A line in the poem reads *"Elected regimes of smart tyrants, Plot wars for bogey speculative interests…"*. The modern state, as many democrats would have us believe, is much more advanced than the old tyrannical regimes of monarchs and emperors. Yet some of the crimes that a few elected regimes today carry out will shame those old tyrants. Violence is veiled in democracy and buried in diplomacy for elected tyrants to whip up nationalistic hysteria to pillage and plunder other nations and minorities.

*28.* First Love (Or Mums so Beloved) : "*Beautiful mums, oft we fail to say so while she's living…"*. How many of us say to our mums how much we love them when they are alive? This is a poem again to appreciate the love of a mother.

*29.* Five Elements: A love poem built around fire, earth, sky, water and air. The poem invokes the five elements for a poetical discourse.

*30.* Fountains of Poetry: Often one wonders from where the poetry originates. This poem is attempting to find some answers to this very pertinent question. "Feeding mum's face aglow, (mother's) breast swells for milk to flow, Soul aches for lullabies to stream, For a baby in a mother's bosom, That is fountain of poetry…"

*31.* Friendly Farewell: "*Friends, time with you around, Grinding slowly to an end…"* reads the first line of the poem. It is a farewell poem to friends. Emotions reach to their peak with lines like "Plentiful joy you brought my way, Enriching my days to heavenly joy.."

*32.* Full Moon and Monsoon Wind: *Mountainous waves rush to stranded shores, Diligent fishermen, sail to sea adjusting the sails…"* reads a line in the poem. The poem is about a beach scene in full moon when the monsoon wind is in full force.

*33.* God's Children Living by Wastelands: On this earth of affluence, many children still live on wastelands. Poverty in its cruel twist makes them roam these wastelands for a pitiful living.

*34.* Greek Tragedy: *"From times of antiquity, flourished your enquiring thirst, Today though, changed times burden your economy to burst…"* The poem wonders what happened to the Greece of great philosophers who wrote classics about virtually everything from politics to poetry, money, philosophy and religion. Such past greatness will not stand in good stead for its current severe financial and economic woes.

*35.* Hate: Often I wonder whether a genetic code has been seeded in humans for their undoing. *"Hate, erase villages in fireball bombs, Hate, end nations in war storms .."* Hate becomes the hidden agent of religious fanatics, extremists in political colours, racial and caste supremacists.

*36.* Heart: This is a poem about the merciful role of the heart in keeping humans alive while the rest of the organs have given up. On a hospital visit to see an uncle of my friend and grandfather of my daughter-in-law, I saw the last gasp struggle of the heart. While being at the verge of entering the gates of All-Souls-Land and yet grasping the robe of life, the heart's final hour of glory was all too evident from the heaves of the heart –the sheer struggle - to hold the breath for a few more moments.

*37.* Wish I Told you Before, Papa: *"Oft in sleep, I sensed your body odour, As I woke, I glimpsed your shadows by the door..."* A poem exploring through the ages a father–son or father-daughter relationship.

*38.* Hunger: "*Affluence hides in shame, Rich all should take blame, Radicals may set the world aflame, As hunger in the world beyond norm...*" A news report caught my eye that more than 1.2-billion of the 7-billion total world population goes hungry every day. What a tragedy! While sky-high towers rise to pronounce the wealth of nations, a good proportion of the world population (nearly 10–15%) goes hungry every day. I got provoked by such shameful statistics and the result is this poem.

*39.* Inspiration: Inspiration arrives in many forms to individuals to be creative in all endeavours in which they are engaged. *" The warmth of your smile, Refreshed me from a mile..."* The poem is a dedication to friends who inspired the writer in several ways.

*40.* So don't weep, Ma, I sleep Peaceful: Ben Kinsella was the inspiration to write this poem. Ben was knifed in June 2008 and having three sons of my own, that triggered me to write this poem. Knife crime lies in the background of the poem. *"Friendly fun drove me to the bar, Villain's knife pierced me to a deep gore..."*

*41.* In Your Golden Hearts: A poem in dedication to Jordan Rice and Irena Sendler. Jordan, a 13 year old boy, who sacrificed his life to save his brother Blake in Queensland's flood and Irena, a Polish Resistance member in occupied Warsaw, who helped to save 2,500 Jewish children from the ghetto, keeping them alive in secret hide-outs. Jordan was a child and Irena, a mature woman with age no bar to having a golden heart. A couplet in the poem reads *"Angels of triumphal spirit, Drop by in twilight moment..."*.

*42.* Life Spectrums: This is a philosophical and poetical discourse on one's life. "*Bound in a miracle confinement, Begins the journey of to-be-born....*".

*43.* Travel of a Baby Cloud: The fond memories of my home village generate a constant ache in my soul. Its current status as a war-ravaged wasteland, robbed of its colours and vibrancy, and the never-escaping pain of not being able to go back to see it as it was once, lie deep in the sentiments of the poem. The poem, written from a baby cloud's perspective, revisits the land having seen its past glory.

*Emotions peak, my eyes sore, tears spill*
*Ever there a place to end my sky bound travel,*
*Here it is, over the land that nourished me well.*
*So I descend, to die as rain drops on the very soil*
*I took birth, so bless me god and bless all people of this soil!*

*44.* Lonely and Starving at Christmas: The poem draws a parable between the festive moods of one home with the deprived state of another.

*45.* Love You All: *"Heart feels heavy with your memories, Hurt I'm for pricking your souls at times..."* A true friend who is remorseful would beg for forgiveness and this poem paints such emotions.

*46.* Mines of Archaic Chill: Chile's mine disaster, which almost killed 33 miners, caught my poetic impulses and bore this poem entitled '*Mines of Archaic Chill*'. The starting lines read like this: *"Craving tummy, screaming poverty, down men into depth of earth's cavity, Striving to scratch a pitiful living; this drove 33 men to the point of dying…"*

*47.* Oh! Magnificent Taj Mahal: This poem is written about an imagined visit by an old man who once visited Taj Mahal with his lover and made a promise to make another trip, but regrettably his lover/wife is no more when he visits the magnificent monument of love this time. *"Many summers passed whence I was here, Maiden who adorned my young shoulder, Moon of my romantic castle no more near…"*

*48.* Mum, A Bouquet at Your Feet: A soulful tribute to my mother on the day of her last journey into the unknown.

*49.* Roads I travelled and My Roots*:* At certain points in time the twists and turns of life make one feel devoid of both the origin and destiny. Especially when one gets uprooted willingly or unwillingly, or a combination of both, the sense of loss is overwhelming. This poem was written when I myself was experiencing such despairing emotions. A line in the poem says it well: *"Neither have I roots nor roads to origin, None to claim as kith or kin…"*

*50.* My Tormented Soul: A poem exploring the emotions of a lover. The verses speak better than my introduction. *"Yesterday seems your presence by my side, Yearning long years since ran beneath the bridge, Waning seasons haven't triggered memories to slide, Woven strings of our past remain highest ridge, Which I can never cross until my tormented soul leaves my cage…"*

*51.* Wounded Heart: A poem of a broken-hearted man. *"Burning amber inner chambers of my soul, Confine grief there I for a new beginning, Yet memories of you and times will remain in my heart forever darling. Friend you have found I hope, Bring all that you wished for…"*

*52.* Nowhere to Hide This Shame: A rebellious poem about poverty and how the world is trying to address this issue. *"Never you witness them (poor) opening their palms, nor do they survive by the meagre alms, thrown their way, not to them, but to the agents of development scam…"*

*53.* Oh Community of Nations: The poem is an outcry at the intransigent stand of developed nations on rights violations by state organs. Intricacies and complexities involved over such actions or inactions are often unexplained. Even when there is compelling evidence over rights violations, they are ignored often for too long by democratically advanced nations. The institutions created internationally to protect the rights of individuals, minorities and the media are of little leverage to prevent abuse. The result is mass violation, death and destruction.

*54.* Oh Gods – Why You Still Hide*: Still schools get bombed, assembly for prayers get torched. Death by remote destruction without trace - the assassins in the name of Gods still march on while preaching godly love on one hand and blowing away lives with another.* The verses put the religious mobs on the defensive, accusing them of the same bigotry of their forefathers.

*55.* Oh the West Bound Winds of Monsson: A sixty year struggle for political freedom against an unjust and brutal regime ended in a tragedy thanks to the World Powers' inaction; resulting in more than forty thousand civilians dying in the last days of the war in Sri Lanka. This poem is a dedication to the civilians killed in the war for liberation. *"Oh the west-bound winds of moist, Do sprinkle drops of tears on our bravest, Whom to the paradise gate we hoist..."*

*56.* Parade on Inhumanity Street: For resisting their advances, a lower caste girl was stripped and chased naked in a street in India by the upper caste men. The shameful thing was other men and women stood and watched this horror. For such an arrogant attack on a defenceless woman, all men must take the blame and be ashamed. "*Stripping and chasing women in open - an extreme cruelty, Could culprits wish such an act on their mother or deity...*"

*57.* Rain Drops on My Grave: For some time it was my desire to write a poem beyond the grave which tackles some of the artificiality of life while being alive. The result was this poem and the verses I like most in it are as follows: *"Blooming buds of roses left on my grave sides, closer to my soul than your perfumed minds..."*

*58.* Road to Decay: A remorseful son's introspection, in prison, at parents for not guiding him to walk the straight lanes of life. It is wise not to regret life after it had gone wrong and instead get it right while one can. The following lines highlight the plight of the son: *"Six by four feet dark stretch, within it I'm boxed by my own sorrows, Fixed stare at ceiling of cockroaches, what I most do in this hell of rogues..."*

*59.* Roses in Turmoil: *"Bare branches of thorny roses, Bear no strength to look to the skies..."* A poem critically comparing the misery-ridden life of humans lasting years with the short-lived, yet amply enriching, life of roses.

*60.* Rickshaw Man: Rickshaw was a colonial tool, used as a means of transport and as a status symbol. Yet even today, it is a means of transport in former colonies, often pulling a family of four or five through crowded streets or unpaved lanes with enormous physical strain. The struggle of a man to make a living out of a rickshaw reveals in its potent entirety the level of poverty when one takes a ride on a rickshaw, yet a working man's pride is his only shining jewel.

*"Slum shack of darkness his abode*
*Gloom and doom inheritance taken on his stride*
*Crumbs in his mud bowl well earned so he's proud*
*Dreams to despair, cohabit in his shack,*
*Yet neither he yawns nor broods*

*61.* Shy Are You: An intimate exchange of poetic thoughts with the full moon being the star of the poetry.

*62.* So Why Weep Mamma?: Battlefields the world over see young men and women giving their lives for government-instigated wars or for rebellious causes. Often these foot soldiers ask no questions about the morality of the war they fight and many die even without grasping the reasons for fighting a war. Yet they embrace death with pride and honour. This poem explores some of the intricate personal feelings of a fighter in the form of a posthumous letter sent to his mother. No mother is ever consoled over the grief of her child's death as that pain is permanent. *"Right must prevail, So we fought and fell..."*

*63.* Against Bullying: A poetic perspective on the inner aching of a bullied child. *Pray to you (God) and humbly plead, Strayed I unknowingly into this world of hate bordering insanity…"*

*64.* Affectionate Affusion (*Thalaikoothal*): A poignant poem on the plight of elderly in the hands of offsprings in some rural villages of India. In circumstances very strange to establish the very thin margin between death by design and display of devotion; a strange bath is given to the elderly who never recover from it. *"An oil bath to end aged misery, Affectionately done, no one is sorry.."*

*65.* Credit Crunch – Spring 2009: *Banks several folded in a debt rush, Yet the ranks of CEO bunch, Collected millions bonuses afresh…"* One of the time traveller's observant notes on the credit crunch in 2009.

*66.* The Last Despatch – A Eulogy to Marie Colvin, *The Times* journalist who covered the most brutal war fronts of the 20th and 21st century including the Balkans, Sri Lanka, Libya and Syria. Her last despatch before her death on 22 February 2012 was from Homs, Syria on 18th February. *"Personified she, the unrelenting spirit, For unearthing the ordinary peoples plight…"* read the lines in the poem. This is a poem in dedication to her professionalism and dedication to the welfare of women and children caught in terrible situations in war zones.

*67.* The Girl of My Dreams: This is a poem dedicated to my high school dream girl who

triggered poetry into my teenage senses. *"White uniform rests gently on her contour, Bright red school tie dangle on her bosom…"* The poem stems from the vivid memories I still have of her.

*68.* The Last Farewell: A funeral is always a solemn moment full of grief and agony. This poem was written soon after the funeral of my friend's uncle and grandfather of my daughter-in-law. *"Entered the remains of the soul departed, with wreaths of love on coffin mounted…"*

*69.* The Lioness of Myanmar: This poem is about a woman of courage and fortitude who spent years in prison for the liberation of her people and the country from the blood-soaked clutches of military dictators of Myanmar. Yes Aung Saan Suu Kyi – the lioness of Myanmar.

*Jason*

*70.* The Ultimate Sacrifice: A humble offering to honour the thousands of young lives lost in Sri Lanka's civil war due to the intransigent and uncompromising stands taken by the Sri Lankan rulers for the last sixty-odd years.

*Virulent winds of violence,*
*Turbulent acts of intolerance,*
*Turned a nation of spiritual peace,*
*Into an army of honour-bound resistance*

*71.* God's Children Living By Wastelands: Poverty pushes children into wastelands in search of disposed food as scavenging is too harsh a word to describe their deprived status. "*Not apple tart they seek, subtle sympathy would do, Little of what you feed your dogs, could go long to settle their disputes…*"

*72.* War Crimes Day – 18th May: A war crime was perfectly staged with the blinds drawn to block the view of the carnage from the international community. A nation of Tamils in Sri Lanka, who became victims of British colonial juggleries, found themselves in an unhappy union and fought honourably through democratic means to undo the mistake. Having failed, they took up armed resistance to liberate themselves for thirty-odd years before being violently put down by the Sri Lankan State. The UK's Channel 4 documentaries of 2011 and 2012 brought this 21st century war crime out into the open.

*73.* Widows of War: Often the cries of widows from war fronts are never heard afar. This poem is dedicated to war widows who silently suffer the ultimate terror at the hands of warring factions.

*Hands of evil, embraced us en mass*
*Passion of death, forced entry into our homes*
*Reason slept fast, while right got raped*
*Treason against human dignity silently staged*
*Who is there to hear us? We're widows of War*

*74.* A Loving Grandpa: A tributary poem to an old man – like many in the world – who, for the sake of their children, even in their advanced old age, still take charge of their grandchildren out of love – like my own grandfather did.

*75.* Writings on the Walls: A critical poem on elections and pledges during the last election in the UK.

*76.* Your Honour: A woman who got pregnant through a rape by armed personnel in Sri Lanka, in protest refused to accept the newborn baby, stating in a court that it was the state that should take charge of her baby. A very moving plea - poem - representing reason and the sentiments of a rights-abused woman.

*77.* Ode on Freedom: "*Hail loud all beings...Its (freedom's) glory so prime, .Flame of freedom held high with blood ...*" These are some highlights of the poem. The poem proudly pronounces the glory of freedom.

*78.* The End Inside: The poem was written soon after learning the serious nature of the illness of a friend. Poetry never dies and yet the person who writes never lives forever. The reality of that end within which triggered this poem - "The End Inside" The last stanza reads : *"The end after all is permanent, Embracing it early or late is destiny, Prefaced to be gay to end in tragedy, That is life in its plumb predicament"*

ND - #0253 - 080726 - C0 - 197/132/11 - PB - 9781780353937 - Gloss Lamination